CRIME FICTION

CRIME FICTION

UEA MA
Creative Writing Anthologies
2024

CONTENTS

LOUISE DOUGHTY Foreword		VII
HENRY SUTTON Introduction		IX
AUSTEN ATKINSON (LEE ARROWSMITH) Wrong Way to Hell		2
KATE BAILEY The Hunters		16
DENISE BENNETT The Ravenous Tiger		28
ELLE BLAIR Adrift		40
G. M. CHIVES The Bee Van		52
SHEENA COOK Men Would Kill For This		64
BENJAMIN DAVIES They Moved Away the Highway		76
RICHARD JERRAM The Makoto Murders		88
VALERIE MCGUIRE Oil and Wine		98
BRIAN MEECHAN While We Slept		108
ELAINE RUBY At Sea in Madrid		120
VAN STANLEY Egg County		132
JESSICA TOSELAND Bodies at the Crown		142
Acknowledgements		154

LOUISE DOUGHTY
Foreword

'The English may not always be the best writers in the world,' said Raymond Chandler, 'but they are incomparably the best dull writers.' Ouch.

Chandler was referring to the so-called Golden Age that included Agatha Christie and Dorothy L Sayers and – implausibly enough – AA Milne, but he had an axe to grind (or should that be, a knife to sharpen?). The mid-century blossoming of crime writing on his side of the big blue pond consisted of hardboiled chaps in his shape, Dashiell Hammet, James M Cain and so on, and he was constitutionally ill-inclined towards the comparatively decorous writers on this side – if you can call anyone decorous when they like inventing ingenious ways to kill people, that is. In *The Simple Art of Murder*, his famous essay, he has great fun with the country home inhabitants of Golden Age crime and its imitators in Cape Cod summer colonies, '[sitting] around sipping Singapore slings and sneering at each other, while the flatfeet crawl to and fro under the Persian rugs, with their Derby hats on.' But if the classic English mystery and its global progeny could be accused of having an unrealistic number of enclosed worlds – manor houses, small villages – one may observe that hardboiled crime is obsessed with gritty underbellies inhabited by detectives with their ties askew and serial killers who enjoy graphic dismemberment but hey, nobody's perfect.

The way in which crime fiction reflects the social mores and preoccupations of any given nation is a subject far too fascinating for the space available here, but I can't help wondering what Chandler would make of today's glorious, kaleidoscopic crime and thriller world – for if the generalisations of the past were on shaky ground back then, they have zero validity now. The genre has exploded. It encompasses cozy crime – and yes, serial killers – but also domestic noir, finely tuned psychological investigation, courtroom dramas, spy stories, cyber punk crime, dystopias. The joy of it lies in its elasticity. We're all crime writers now: and it really does feel as though there's never been a better time to be one.

In the pages of this anthology, you will find the classic writers of the future, along with a highly entertaining display of that shape-shifting kaleidoscope. The current crop of MA in Crime Writing students at UEA are writing books set all over the world, on cruise ships, remote farms, dilapidated hotels, in every kind of style and with every sense of adventure: these are writers who are fearless and ambitious and obey no boundaries in what they do. The best of luck to them as they enter the bear pit of the publishing world: a writer's life can be pretty cut-throat off the page as well as on, after all, but on the evidence of the boldness demonstrated here I would venture even the cynical Chandler would have felt the future to be in safe hands.

    Louise Doughty
    London, June 2024

HENRY SUTTON
Introduction

By their very nature, introductions to such anthologies require a certain amount of looking back. In this instance, I'm looking back over two extraordinary years. Coming out of COVID, the Queen dying on the first day of the course, a couple more useless prime ministers, and finally an end in sight to the domestic chaos, and appalling lack of government care and support for the arts and creativity. Yet, throughout this time, I personally have been very greatly creatively, academically and socially sustained and fulfilled by the dedication, talent, insightfulness, critical acumen, wise counsel, cohesion, good humour, and of course the wildly varied, ambitious and inclusive crime stories that the writers in this collection have developed. Truly, they have taken the MA to even greater places, by pushing literary boundaries, challenging preconceptions, demonstrating the endless ways to engage and entertain, to inform, express and enable audiences wide and large.

The Crime Fiction MA is premised on two key concepts – questioning what such a genre is and can be, and generating a novel to explore and illustrate an answer. That answer might well be a further question, of course. And questions, as we know, are foundational to generating mystery and suspense. Novels that actually work, on their own terms, are really difficult to conceive and write. Novels that are steeped in purpose, pace, drama, clear and clever design; menace and motivation, also, if you wish, are arguably even harder to create. This is where form meets function, and literary pretension, or writing for writing's sake, is left outside.

The writers in this anthology have spent the last two years developing the voices of their novels, the stories they want their characters to tell, the worlds they want them to inhabit, destabilise, transgress, and, occasionally, reform and reconstruct. These are clever novels, well written, planned, deeply considered, sometimes challenging, sometimes surprising, ever enlightening. All deserve attention, not least because they question the foundations of genre, the crime genre, and what the novel can do, and where it can go. This is where we begin to look forward, to these stories gaining traction out in the wild, these writers developing their craft, their sensibilities, their publishing careers.

In this collection of beginnings, we begin in the North Sea, a short stretch from Whitby, with prejudices and between-war passions already boiling (*Wrong Way to Hell*). We move to a future time, but where old passions can still be lethal, and familial secrets and ties darkly binding (*The Hunters*). Another step into the near future finds us in a partly destroyed London, and a reimagined Shakespearean tragedy, every bit as violent and disturbing as *Titus Andronicus* (*The Ravenous Tiger*).

A cruise with her family might be just the thing a feisty, suspended detective needs, but nothing could be more lethally disturbing, and darkly humorous, than a week of all you can eat luxury on the high seas (*Adrift*). Meanwhile, a breath of fresh Italian riviera air might provide some comfort, along with spectacular sea and mountainous views, but one woman's struggle to find the truth about her family, and former community, only unearths even more murderous historical actions (*The Bee Van*). Rural Scotland, likewise, appears full of familial dysfunction, and shocking sibling rivalry, despite a remote rural setting and deeply lyrical prose, in a tale that asks stark questions about identity and belonging (*Men Would Kill For This*). Identity is also a major theme for a Los Angeles based drama featuring a cult, a conman, a determined female cop and a failing journalist, one of whom is a serial killer (*They Moved Away the Highway*). The killer at the heart of a particularly twisty Japanese-based murder mystery, which centres on photographic evidence and provocation, says as much about the perpetrator as the viewer (*The Makoto Murders*).

Corruption of a different kind comes under the scrutiny of freelance investigative reporter Flaminia, in southern Italy, a beautiful cultural landscape desecrated by people traffickers and duplicity (*Oil and Wine*). Colder and rougher environments, Glasgow in 1979 and 2010, feature in a politically charged thriller, where personal and public lives collide in love, desire and catastrophe (*While We Slept*). While Madrid provides a brighter setting in a complex conspiracy involving property, the protagonists have far darker and more complicit sides, in a thriller that leaves the biggest twist until the very end (*At Sea in Madrid*).

Neurodiversity is delicately and devastatingly portrayed in a gothic noir set in the southern US (*Egg County*). Also playing on the gothic, and the uncanny, is an inspired country house hotel murder mystery, where the real perpetrator is far more pernicious, persistent and creative than mere mortals could ever attain to be (*Bodies at the Crown*). Or is that quite the case?

Things are not what they seem, is a phrase variously attributed to Jim Thompson. In this collection you will be surprised, startled, enlightened and entertained. This is broad-reaching, intelligent work, which attests to the dynamism and depth of the crime fiction genre. While the work interrogates the past, and previous forms, these extracts, from completed novels, show brilliant ways forward, and demand attention from wide audiences. I'm immensely proud of these novels, these writers, all that they have achieved so far, and can't wait to see where they go next.

Henry Sutton
Professor of Creative Writing and Crime Fiction
Director, Creative Writing MA Crime Fiction
UEA
June 2024

This eclectic anthology showcases 5,000 words of each novel created by the writers completing from UEA's renowned Crime Writing MA course in 2024.

AUSTEN ATKINSON
WRITING AS LEE ARROWSMITH

Austen started writing for Marvel Comics aged 15. Now 54, he is an award-winning executive producer and writer/director in TV. His work as Google project lead on immersive technologies took him into intelligence agency and smart city projects, unearthing lots of material for crime novels.

austen.atkinson@gmail.com

Wrong Way to Hell

The opening of a novel

CHAPTER ONE

The North Sea, 2.45 am, Wednesday, October 30th 1929

Salt bit Obadiah Hack's face. Fists of air and ocean pummelled his oil-skinned body. He clung to the ship's wheel, feeling the rhythm. Judging the moment, he turned her into the wave. He narrowed his eyes, lines around them so deep they made him look like Old Father Time, so his Missus told him. They were slits in a face hidden beneath a red-grey beard and a black salt and sweat stained oilskin fishing hat. Keyed-up and wily, he searched for tells written in the environment. The night sky was ash grey. Low-lying dirty clouds swam across the moon at nigh on twenty knots. Hard a'port he saw waves whipped into a deadly glossy wall. In barely a moment, winds switched from off the land to off the sea. Obadiah knew the lay of things at Twelve-Mile Banks near Whitby. They were in trouble.

He'd hoped for a good catch. He habitually fished at night, many of his kindred disagreed with the method, not least his own boy and grandson, who were moaning more and more about his old ways, these days. For him, night-time was when he was most likely to win at the chase. Fish felt safe and came from the lower depths more than they were likely to in daylight. He'd always brought the biggest catch to the quay, proved he had a way with these things. Let the youngsters do what they liked. While he was still skipper, night was right.

The net had shot away at thirty fathoms. He'd expected a five-hour drag. Minimum. The storm had ruined it. He cursed old Neptune for being in a hell of a mood.

'Heave up,' he yelled.

His boy and grandson were aft. Unsteady silhouettes pummelled by sledgehammers. The vibrations through the deck told him they'd heard, the low-pressure winch was hauling in on the aft gallows. The net bag emerged, a fleeting glimpse amidst the darkness, its tight hemp weave a mesh of intersecting lines. Gouts of black water cascaded through its openings as it ascended rapidly, swinging erratically in the air. It looked a good haul.

A black thirty-footer right out of nowhere slammed the hull, tossing the groaning boat, ramming the skipper against the wheel's barrel and axle nut. He growled as ribs cracked, making breath hard to come by. He heard the engine judder, its propeller screw spinning in the air as the wave lifted it clear of the water. He waited for his moment. The screw and rudder slammed back into the water. Spinning the wheel, instinctively countering the yaw and pitch, he righted the boat and forced himself to breathe. He snatched a look aft. The wave rushed off the deck leaving two blackened smears clinging to the gunwale. They were there. It hadn't taken his family.

All business, rushing to make safe, his boy timed the swing of the bag and his grandson released the codend. Judged it well. The catch spewed into the deck pond.

'Dad! Oh my God. Dad!'

The skipper lashed the wheel, then turned to look at his son, who held aloft a hurricane lantern. The deck was slick with retreating sea water, he stumbled, grabbed a handrail. Rib pain seared. Wind lashed. He pulled his oilskin closer, caught his breath, then staggered aft, his left arm curled around his ribs. He stared down at ten kit of fish. Flailing and gasping in the deck pond.

He saw it. They all did. Skipper Obadiah Hack fought to swallow his emotions. His disgust at something already dead. Writhing fish bizarre against its stillness. Naked. Emaciated. A man. A mass of bruises. Ragged holes ripped in his neck. Something small and red on him, in stark contrast to his chalk white skin. The skipper blinked to clear the salt from his eyes. It was a new tattoo. On the dead man's arm. A rose. Red. *Red means dead.*

CHAPTER TWO

Harbour, Whitby, North Yorkshire, 8.07 am, same day

DI Steele hated being late. Especially when Detective Chief Inspector Gallop was on. He slammed the door of his Singer motorcar behind him, flipped down his shirt collar, blessed Gladys for running after him with his tie as he'd left and knotted it as he walked. Ahead, hundreds of people pressed together. Ogling. Hoping for a thrill. There were so many that all he could make out of the Fish Quay was the top third of the masts of the older sailing vessels, bobbing slowly above the heads of onlookers. The volume of the crowd's chatter was astonishing. Like being at a funfair. Not for the first time Steele remarked to himself that the ordinarily reserved Brits loved rubbernecking around something grisly. He pushed his way through, annoyed. Six deep, he finally found the police cordon. Dozens of constables forming a line of blue felted wool and leather.

'Jennings,' Steele hissed under his breath at one of the young police constables holding the press and thronging crowd back, 'this is a bloody shambles. Move this lot back fifty yards.'

'We did try, sir.' Jennings was a hopeful but hopeless case. Destined to get fat and ride a bike. Smiling at tourists for the next thirty years.

'Just do it. And for goodness' sake lad, straighten yer helmet. Did your mother forget to wipe your arse as well?' Steele pushed passed him, giving the hardest stare that he reserved for particularly dumb individuals. He cut through the human cordon of perhaps thirty constables. The stench of wet fish and brine was sharp.

He saw the rest of the bobbing masts, like heads of corn dancing in the wind. Five purposeful uniformed and plain-clothed people doing dark tasks were concentrated around one of the masts. Steele walked to the edge of the quay and looked down into the boat they were on.

Chief Inspector Gallop was one of the five. He looked up at Steele. 'Jesus, Jack, where the hell have you been this time?' He was a weary grey-haired man. In his late fifties. A ruddy complexion. Carrying a little too much weight. Gallop's tailor would have cried at the strain that his pin stripe suit was under.

'This time?'

Gallop dismissed the customary Steelian games with a wave of his hand. 'Show Detective Inspector Steele, please Doctor.'

Steele looked down. A withered naked corpse with paper-thin white skin was curled in the foetal position, on the trawlerman's working deck. A short round middle-aged man was examining the body.

Steele was revulsed. Felt acid in his throat.

'Aye. It's him at it again,' Gallop took a drag on his pipe and exhaled a gout of smoke. 'I'm telling you, this is beyond our pay grade.'

'We can handle it.'

'For Christ's sake, the whole bloody town's up in arms. The Chief wants us to get Sir Bernard Spilsbury.'

Steele scowled. 'The Crippen guy?'

'Right. He's a pain in the arse.' Gallop's pipe glowed red.

'You'll love him then.'

Gallop exhaled, meaningfully. 'And too expensive.'

Steele climbed aboard. 'You get what you pay for. You're a case in point.'

'You're all heart, Jack.'

Doctor Bartholomew Harris, generally referred to as Old Bart, was North Yorkshire Police's Medical Examiner. A florid fastidious little bald man, round in all ways, and sporting significant salt and pepper sideburns, he finished his initial examination. He tilted the victim's head, skin white as paper, the neck stick-thin against his own pudgy hand. 'You see the bruising on the neck?'

Steele nodded. He felt the bile in his throat burbling as he looked down at the Doctor handling the corpse. He didn't think he'd ever get used to seeing the murdered.

'It seems to be from multiple incidents.'

'Incidents? You mean beatings?' Steele asked.

'Cannulas, well, large gauge needles,' the Doctor said.

'That's familiar,' Steele glanced at Gallop who nodded and then back at Old Bart. 'Would they cause that level of bruising?'

'No. It seems purposeful. It's just my opinion, but I think he's torturing the victims as he bleeds them.' The Doctor looked between Steele and Gallop, challengingly.

Steele was silent.

Gallop looked at him. 'You'd better send for that foreign lad.'

Steele scowled. 'Who, now?'

'The bloke from the papers. Y'know, you worked with him. Oh, for god's sake Jack, that mulato lad. The press call him the Murder Man.'

'Lavant?'

'Aye.'

'He's an awkward bugger an'all. He's not foreign. He's a Geordie.'

'Bloody clever, I hear.'

Steele was silent.

Telegram from Det Inspector Jack Steele, N. Riding Police Force to Roche Lavant, Police Science Investigations Ltd, 30th Oct. 1929.

POST OFFICE TELEGRAM
| No. 545

	Charge to Pay	*Office Stamp*
To: Roche Lavant 9 Ellison Place, Newcastle Upon Tyne	3s4d	Newcastle Upon Tyne
Handed in at: Whitby	at 9.04 a.m.	Received at: 09.21 a.m.

Strictest Confidence STOP Roche Lavant's services required STOP Ongoing Whitby murder investigation needs police science to break deadlock STOP Exsanguinated body found in sea today STOP Sixth body to date STOP Red rose tattoo STOP Contract for you and team offered on same terms as Newcastle Force STOP Come at once STOP Jack Steele STOP

CHAPTER THREE

Crime Room, Literary & Philosophical Society, Newcastle Upon Tyne, 9.38 am, Same Day.

The pensive boy pulled his tunic down and tugged his hat's peak a little lower. He walked through the high archway into the library's Crime Room and hesitated. He looked around but couldn't see his target.

It was a large square room. Windows high up on his left. Focused light pouring down through them in blocks, like the fingers of God, warming squares of green parquet flooring. Bookcases were arrayed around the cream walls and at right angles into the room. Crammed full. Thousands of books of every colour. Only the domed ceiling and high windows were bookless. He savoured the smell of old paper, rubbed leather and well-read ink.

'Up here, Jimmy. Got something for me?'

The telegram boy pivoted, looking for the owner of the voice from above. Craning his neck, he found him on the mezzanine, behind him. Turning, he took in the man he had come to find. Roche Lavant walked deftly down the tight red and black wrought iron spiral staircase. He was a blur of cravat, pinstripe pants, silk tape-edged black jacket, grey waistcoat and well-used boots. Lean, fit, not handsome, not ugly, a face unfinished but one that made an impression. The smile that everyone loved was an ear-to-ear half circle. The pencil line moustache gave him the rake look that seemed to suit the newspapers. His skin glowed like burnished bronze. Jimmy felt dull next to him.

'Yes sir. It's a priority message, Mister Lavant,' the boy said, standing to attention.

Lavant waved him over to a table, one of six in a row in the reading room of the Lit and Phil Library, as it was known. The oldest and largest library outside of London, and Lavant's usual haunt.

Lavant stared down at the desk. *The Times* newspaper was open at page 11. A red circle demarked an article.

The telegram boy pulled a message from his small leather belt pouch and handed it over. 'I think it's important sir.'

'No doubt. You seen this, Jimmy?' Lavant asked, tapping the newspaper.

'No, sir. You in the papers again?'

'Terrible business on Wall Street.'

'London, sir?'

'New York. Millions of dollars wiped out.'

'Won't affect us though, sir, surely.'

'I had money invested in a bank. They're building a new sky-high development in Manhattan.'

'I didn't even know you could do that, sir.'

'Me either. I wish I still didn't. The project director just jumped off the twenty-eighth floor,' he said tapping the article, 'and he's not alone.'

'Sorry to hear that, sir. That why you ringed it? Worried like?'

'I didn't. Someone else was worried. Maybe we all should be.'

Lavant's attention was gone, his focus pulled by the scrap of paper that Jimmy had given him. He read it twice. Jimmy watched his eyes moving. Narrowing.

'D'you see Mister Dawson in the city?' Lavant asked.

'Yes sir. He's got his easel set up, doing a painting at the new bridge.'

'Get him for me, would you? Tell him to pack a bag for, say, fourteen nights away.'

'Should he meet you at Central Station?'

Lavant smiled. 'Please. In an hour.'

'You want me to tell Mister Samuelson and Missus Dunham?'

Lavant nodded. 'They'll be at Swinburne Place. Best tell them to do likewise.'

Jimmy was already moving off.

'Jimmy, tell them to pack the kit. All of it. And please ask Mrs Dunham to pack my old service revolver and her Lee Enfield.'

'Divn't worry sir.' Jimmy stopped and spun on his heels. 'Sorry sir, I forgot. Any reply?'

Lavant looked down at the telegram. 'Good lad, thank you, yes. Say…' Lavant waited for Jimmy to pull his chitty book and pencil, 'Message received STOP Team and I will come at once STOP Move nothing STOP Lavant STOP. That's twelve words, right? One shilling, isn't it?'

'Yes sir.'

Lavant patted his pockets. Empty. He looked at Jimmy. Jimmy looked at Lavant. Lavant smiled and pulled his watch chain from his waistcoat pocket. He detached a golden coin and flicked it to Jimmy.

'A sovereign sir?' Jimmy felt a thrill go through him as he stared at it in the palm of his hand.

'Didn't pay you last month, did I? Better make that last.'

'Yes, sir, if you're sure, sir. Thank you, Mister Lavant, sir.'

Lavant wasn't listening. The boy saw Lavant's keen dark eyes dart to the thousands of volumes on the crime mezzanine above him. Jimmy smiled and tapped the brim of his hat. As he left, Jimmy heard him mutter, 'Need books on Whitby and tattoos.'

TELEGRAMM

Absender Kosten Büro
Herr Roche Lavant | 5 schilling | Wien

Adresse Datum
Büro von Dr. Johannes Schober 30. Oktober 1929
Internationale Polizeikommission, Wien

Ort der Übermittlung: Newcastle Großbritannien | **at** 10.25 a.m. | **Erhalten:** 11.33 a.m.

Geheimtext: fcle99pn9gkkqxvffyfjyl2b9cgknjhg9knncocxetpxsdbri2cd2ihaanhqmmmhhvxtj9oga9isjysvatktb2df2schkekfowrgvfsgemacmpadbcsr9nfhtgqinaa9htumsyjuooyldichlmdyndlijofo2dtxpecyabwllwooi9iqllxdfscaibchdjumsyjwbm9kkksax2cuaebxmk9lgi9aitdushkim9iprgqmfvmjmhi9vtoqboewwgligvvfbtqvswhsppidgeawjicoiwdjwnsxbujicalrqa2oeayekvfssrqxxagvl9

[Telegram decoded by Dr Johannes Schober, Chief, International Criminal Police Commission (ICPC), Vienna. Encrypted with Standard ICPC Trifid Cipher / Key: CRIME29 / Group Size: 5.]

Decoded ciphertext:
Felicitations Johannes STOP Been engaged to bring police science to murder hunt STOP Whitby North Yorkshire England STOP Need ICPC Police network reports of any known criminal movements in vicinity STOP Please send word pictures of any persons of interest STOP Correspond C/O DI Steele N Riding Yorks Constabulary STOP Will report progress to your office in Vienna STOP Lavant STOP

CHAPTER FOUR
Private Compartment, LNER Train, the Hinterland nr. Whitby, 2.57pm, same day

After four hours on a steam train, two brandies against the autumn weather and six games of mah-jong, Roche Lavant suddenly knew he was anxious. Since the horrors of France, he was mindful of his state of being and acted to prevent problems. He stood, walked across the compartment, caught his reflection in the glass. A lean angular face, olive brown skin, quizzical black arrows for brows. A pensive man. He pulled a leather tab in the centre of the outer door, the droplight window slid down. A burst of clattering rail song and salt-laced ozone-sweetened air exhilarated him. He checked for safety and craned out, looking towards the loco, taking a moment to revel in the soft kiss of steam and gentle tap-tap of soot against his face. As he and his three friends were in the frontmost compartment, he was able to see one of the loco's great drive wheels biting at a rail. Polished to a shine by friction, the rail was a dart, stretching ahead, beyond the green gold of the loco's body. He felt a shudder through the floor plates as it changed gait, dropping from gallop to canter.

Lavant noted that dusk was closing in. Rendering near-empty moors as inky mesas. Iridescent boulder lichen traceries and highlight-crowned hedgerows were stretched by the loco's forward motion, becoming smudged brush strokes from a Turner painting. He felt anticipation rip through him as he caught his first glimpse of the town. A growing island of light in a sea of twilight. He had the impression of hard linear structures, black cut-outs jutting up.

After a blur of sidings and points, the train darted between the legs of a giant viaduct and was, as if crossing a meniscus, enveloped by haze. Lavant glimpsed a cat's cradle of streets, the haze was like gossamer silk spun between sentinel glow-worm gas lamps dotted across the town. Some lamps close enough to touch, others distant glimmers.

Whitby station, a brick, wrought iron and glass affair, seemed like a mouth opening to swallow them. Lavant caught sight of their final destination in staccato glimpses. The harbour was crammed with twitching hats and furled collars.

Dozens of shining stars. Not in the heavens but fixed to blue pointed custodian helmets worn by massed police constables. A blue human barrier holding back a crowd. Beyond them all, a sense of focus. Bobbing masts, two hundred yards from the station, drawing the attention of the large semi-circular sea of onlookers. The fishing boat, he concluded. Innocuous from afar.

Lavant caught a stream of movement, a human riptide cutting through the onlookers. Trilbies and homburgs, great coats, and black and silver boxes with bellows, hustling for the station's steps. Reporters. Summoned by the throaty huffing of their steam engine.

Lavant turned to Mary Dunham. 'Looks like you're going to be busy keeping that lot distracted.'

Mary looked up. 'Operation filibuster.'

Lavant smiled at her. 'Right.' He watched her mercurial face for a moment. She was reading him. He knew he'd be lost if she didn't keep him organised.

Mary, an elfin French-bobbed brunette, looked diminutive, sat beside their bear of a friend, sketch artist Byron Dawson. Scene of crime photographer Henry Samuelson, a boyish bantamweight, faired little better in comparison to the Bear. Dawson and Mary were deep into the hefty ABC Railway guide, looking for suitable accommodation in Whitby. Samuelson was cleaning a lens for one of the team's cameras.

Lavant turned to Samuelson. 'The harbour seems pretty well lit. Maybe you'll be alright with a fine-grained emulsion.'

Samuelson put down his lens and walked to stare out of the window. 'Aye, divn't suppose our victim'll be dancing about. I've done up some of the new infra-red plates for the camera, too.'

Lavant nodded. 'That'll be fascinating.'

'Should give us an edge on anything their police surgeon has up his sleeve,' Samuelson said.

'Might surprise us,' Mary said, joining them at the compartment's door.

Samuelson snorted. 'Howay man. Fiver says they've got a total fool.'

'Better a witty fool than a foolish wit,' Dawson said from behind them, sidling up to join his friends.

Mary glanced at Samuelson. 'They've shown some class, they've hired us, haven't they?'

'True,' Samuelson said.

Lavant was silent as he thought about interacting with the local police MD. They were usually strong-stomached doctors approaching retirement. Picking up fees from legitimate second jobs as expert witnesses. Lavant hoped for a warm welcome but rarely got it. Some were keen to learn from him. Most dismissed him as a busybody foreigner.

'Twenty-six press. Thirty-two constables,' Dawson mumbled.

Mary glanced past Lavant, at Dawson. The four of them were now arrayed along the windows and doorframes of the compartment, staring outwards. 'I'm amazed they can call on that many Bobbies.'

Lavant noticed that Dawson didn't blink. His faculty to remember and draw things after a single glance made him a singular talent for a detective agency. 'Not all the Brunswick stars are the same. On their helmets. Neighbouring forces maybe,' Dawson said.

Mary was astonished. 'You could see that from here?'

Dawson was silent.

Lavant at the window in the outer door, felt the air pressure and quality change on his face as the train slid into Whitby Station. He saw the reporters burst through the station's entrance at a run, the platform beneath their feet smoothed by the motion of the train and persistence of vision. The illusion made them look like overdressed ice-skaters.

Lavant wondered what had tipped the press off about their presence on the train, then he got his answer. Ahead of the journalists, bustling along the platform, Lavant saw a familiar figure. Lean, tall, strident. 'There. Look,' he said, 'that's Steele.' Seeing his old colleague made it all real. No longer an abstract problem.

Lavant saw a pressman pursue the train, run past Inspector Steele and lift a black box, a glass eye on the front, a trough attached to its side. With no time to recoil or gather his wits, a blue-white flare momentarily obscured Lavant's vision as their arrival was immortalised.

Cutting from The Evening Chronicle, 30 October 1929 (pasted in Roche Lavant's journal).

SLAUGHTER IN WHITBY.

Fishing Boat Nets Sixth Body.

POLICE CALL IN MURDER MAN.

Whitby, N. Yorks.

POLICE ARE BAFFLED in the ongoing multiple murder case in Whitby. A sixth body was discovered today by three fishermen. Hauling in their nets early, so as to take shelter in harbour from an unholy storm that lashed the northeast coast this morning, they were shocked to land a human corpse. A naked male, approximately 38 years of age, ghastly pale, clearly bludgeoned and brutalised to death.

Well-known local skipper, Mr Obadiah Hack (67), was at the wheel of his vessel Sweet Jemima as the horrifying catch was dropped onto the deck.

"We was caught up in a big grey-un, had us bobbing about like a cork in a swell. We hauled in and it was my lad Johnny-Jack dropped the catch. Me heart stopped when yon'en whalloped onto the deck. He was all bent, y'know? Sort-a-curled the ways a scared dog'll take to doing. Trying to get all smalled up, like. Died protecting h'self from a whipping, I reckon as not." The victim's face was reportedly contorted into a ghastly shape, as if in fear and pain. "I'll never forget it. Twisted it was. Mark my words, when they catch the wrong'un what done this, he'll be a demon and no mistake," Captain Hack said.

New Police Science From The Murder Man.

Det. Chief Inspector Gallop and Det. Inspector Steele are leading the investigation for North Yorkshire Police. After pressure from locals and rumours of intervention from the Home Office, they have hired Roche Lavant and his team from Police Science Investigations Ltd. of Newcastle-Upon-Tyne. Lavant, referred to as "Murder Man" in the popular press, is a former police detective. He has lately made a name for himself as a leading exponent of the kind of police science that caught Dr Crippen.

"Our job here in Whitby is to bring rationality where there is fear. To apply science and deduction to the baffling and the strange. I promise to do everything in my power to expose and catch the person or persons behind these unspeakable horrors," said Mr Lavant.

CHAPTER FIVE
Harbour, Whitby, North Yorkshire, 3.11 p.m. Same day.

Lavant said a silent prayer for his team. Mary was a trooper, pushing him along the platform, through the squawking press corps. Allowing them to grab a short quote while steering him towards the open doorway.

'Gentlemen! If you could please let Mister Lavant get to work, we're happy to invite you to a press conference this evening…!' She'd thrown the hungry gulls some mackerel to keep them in order enough to get Lavant out of the station. Steele had tried to shake his hand and mumble a strangled hello, but the disorientating hot powder flashes of the photographers and crush of reporters had swept them apart.

Lavant skittered down the station's steps. Unable to see his feet or stonework for the crush of limbs. In a few moments he was across the crowded street and onto the quayside, all the while making for the masts, not a hundred yards away. It was chaos. The townsfolk, not just the reporters, rushed him. Wanting a piece of him. Faces, tall, thin, square. All desperate.

An older lady, a washerwoman he thought, whisky breathed, eyes swollen from crying, pushed rosaries into his hand. 'God bless you, sir. Please, will you help us? Please, sir.'

Other voices swamped him, cacophonous, overlapping. He heard nothing distinct but understood what they were communicating. After six murders and no answers, this town was terrified.

Lavant's head swirled. He felt out of control. Desperate faces, turned up at him, full of impossible expectations. He'd never encountered anything like it. He felt Dawson grab his left arm and Steele take a vice-like grip on the other. Pushing him.

With glimpses of blue woollen tunics, jostling people and flashes of photographers' cameras, Steele and Dawson barged him through the cordon of constables onto the edge of the quay. He stood panting. Steele also. A moment of relief. Steele slapped him on the back. Dawson had let go, vanishing into the crowd. Doing his job, moving amongst them. Looking, listening, sketching. Mary Dunham, he was sure, would play the pied piper. Luring the press to the Royal Hotel.

The Sweet Jemima was a forlorn sight. A small propeller-driven trawler. Her deck pond full of dead, petrol-sheened fish. Curled there, king of the heap, was the victim. Naked. Ashen. His one splash of colour, a ruby red rose tattoo, like a beacon, on his forearm. Here was a lost soul who might tell Lavant everything, if he could just find a way to listen.

'Lavant, this is DCI Gallop.' Steele stepped aboard the Sweet Jemima, pointing at a thickset older man as he did so. Lavant followed, wobbling a little as the trawler pitched and yawed. He got his balance, stood upright and turned to take in Gallop. He was wearing a three-piece pinstripe, felt trilby jammed on his head, with a smouldering pipe jutting from clenched teeth. He was perched on the roof of the wheelhouse. Gallop's dangling feet, and cherubic round face, conjured an image of a naughty kid sitting in a neighbour's tree.

Lavant smiled at him and tapped the brim of his homburg. 'Nice to meet you, sir. I've heard a lot about you.'

Gallop's pipe glowed red, as he sucked on it, an irritated tell that Lavant noted for future reference. Gallop's eyes narrowed a little, dismissively. 'About me? I doubt it. Everyone's forgotten.'

'Not everyone. The King's Police Medal. Not exactly a common award.'

Gallop said nothing.

'And this is Old Bart.., excuse me,' Steele cast a glance at Old Bart, embarrassed, 'Doctor Bartholomew Harris. Dr Harris, this is Roche Lavant. You'll have heard—'

'—I'm the responsible Police Surgeon,' Old Bart said, tilting his head and eyeing Lavant.

Lavant stepped forward and held out his hand, smiling, eyes-on-eyes. He'd anticipated some brace, and he was reading more than he'd have liked.

Old Bart glanced down at Lavant's hand. Was he seriously considering refusing to shake it? Lavant felt his smile widen as he increased his charm quotient. Old Bart glanced at Steele, who Lavant noted had a thunderous expression, then over Lavant's shoulder at Gallop.

Whatever Gallop had gestured, that did it. Old Bart stepped in and shook Lavant's hand. It was awkward, hard, almost crushing. He tried to grind Lavant's knuckles. Pathetic. What is this, junior school? Lavant squeezed back. Hard.

'Yes well, we've all heard about yer fancy ways,' Old Bart said. Lavant noticed his strong Yorkshire twang, and suspected it came out more under emotional duress. 'Nevertheless,' Old Bart gave Lavant a challenging stare, 'I doubt you'll be finding us wanting here lad.' He let go of Lavant's hand. The disengagement was a swipe away. Not so much a polite how-do-you-do, more of a how-do-you-don't.

'Well, my team and I are always happy to support responsible police surgeons,' Lavant didn't break his gaze, 'and sometimes we can bring a few points of difference.'

'Aye, well, we'll not be holding with any of your foreign ways here, lad. Just stick to procedure and we'll get along just fine.'

'Foreign?'

Old Bart was bristling. 'Exotic ideas and all.'

Lavant was silent. He waited for it.

Old Bart's patience snapped, 'We don't need any bloody oomee-gooby-land voodo'ere. Alright?'

'I'm a Geordie. From Newcastle, born there, bred there.'

Lavant pointed at the body in the trawler's fishpond. 'This sixth murder, is it as likely to be solved as the previous five? Or do you think maybe there's some evidence that a fresh pair of eyes might see?'

'Alright gents,' Steele stepped in between them and glowered at Old Bart, who backed off and went into a make-busy-schtick, tapping his pockets, hunting and producing his pack of cigarettes and matches. As Old Bart lit up, Steele glanced apologetically at Lavant. 'Your man there,' he nodded behind Lavant, towards the quayside, 'he's seemingly wanting aboard. Alright with you?'

Lavant broke his gaze from Old Bart and glanced ashore. Samuelson smiled back at him. 'Room for a little one? I reckon we might have a few tricks up our sleeves that'll fair astound even a wise old pro like you, Doc,' Samuelson said, winking, and tapping their boxes of tricks stacked beside him on the quayside. Lavant winked back. He could have kissed him.

***

Thirty highly productive minutes passed. Lavant was finding the weight of expectation, and the hubbub of the townsfolk, on the other side of the police cordon, claustrophobic. With night barely ten minutes out and quayside gas lamps not as abundant as he had hoped, he worked fast.

KATE BAILEY

Kate Bailey studied the Creative Writing Diploma at Oxford University before embarking on the MA in Crime Fiction at UEA. In 2022 she was a LISP short story finalist. She has an interest in exploring how generational stories and self-deception can make people believe the unbelievable. *The Hunters* is her first novel.

katebwriter@hotmail.com
X – @Kate_B_Writer

The Hunters

The opening of a novel

CHAPTER ONE – BENJI

In defiance of the night and the monsters prowling within it, the boy slept. His limbs were thrown about, mouth slightly open, his breath a whistle. He was unaware of the tap on the door downstairs, of the hurried footsteps and swish of clothing, and of the soft click and thud of the door opening and then closing.

It was the candle that stirred him. It flickered in the shifting of air, making the shadows in the room jump and dance. The boy's eyes twitched beneath their lids and his lashes fluttered. He raised a drowsy hand, mumbling under his breath.

'Mama?' he called, croaky and hoarse. He reached out grasping fingers, but met only dead air. He sat up and rubbed his face. Sleep-grit pinched in the corners of his eyes.

He yawned and stretched. The woollen blanket, already half kicked off, flowed to the floor in an itchy pile. Amanda would have said that it was too hot for such a blanket, if she were here. But he couldn't sleep without it. Mama had made it just for him.

'Mama?' Benji called again. His mouth was dry and tasted sour. He took a sip from the small cup of water by his bed. It really was too hot in the room. But every night he insisted that the single window be latched tightly shut, just in case. Amanda had always complained about it, but he would rather they all be too hot, than the alternative.

The candle still flickered on the table by Mama's rocking chair, where night by night she creaked back and forth, mending clothing. In the winter months she would knit, wooden needles clicking and clacking as the fire popped and crackled, humming a soft lullaby.

But tonight, the chair was empty and still.

She was not there.

Benji knew that his Mama would not leave him, not ever. For every night of his seven years, she had sat, rocked and hummed right there. She had worn little grooves in the wooden floor. Smiling small reassurances when he woke in the night; when he cried out in fear of the encroaching dark; tucking his blanket back around him when he would thrash in his sleep.

Yet despite the knowing of all of this, his Mama was still not there.

It was not forbidden to go out after dark. But everyone knew that it was a foolish thing to do. Margaret said that anyone who left in the night would get snatched.

They would get snatched and torn and would be made dead in a way that was worse than anything that you could imagine.

The problem was that Benji could imagine a lot of things.

He swung his legs over the edge of the bed and set his feet on the roughly planked floor. He thought about looking in the shadows under the bed to see whether his Mama might have fallen, might have hit her head and rolled there somehow, but the thought of putting his face or hands near that darkness made him shudder. If there was a monster hiding there, he didn't want to see it.

It wasn't that he was scared of the dark. Not exactly. That was only for babies and wimps. And he was neither.

He crossed the room in just a few steps, standing on the hems of his slightly too long pyjamas and deliberately skirting around the dark places. A small pair of trousers were draped on the rocking chair, a gaping tear halfway down. Mama's needle was still stuck into them, the mending only half finished.

Benji winced and gingerly poked at the matching scab on his knee, traces of pungent ointment still sticky on his skin. He couldn't explain why, even to himself, but the sight of the haphazardly-placed mending bothered him even more than the absence of his mother. Mama always put her work back in the basket - she never left it out where curious hands might pull apart her painstaking work, or get themselves stabbed with the sharp needle, or worst of all - drop it in between the floorboards so that it was lost forever.

He gathered it, sticking himself once with the needle even though he was extra careful, yelping in shock. He turned, arms held out in rigid earnestness, taking small, shuffled steps until he could place it in the basket.

Job done, he tiptoed over to the door. It swung when he touched it, opening into the dark void of the stairwell. He didn't want to go down there, but now that he was fully awake, he needed his Mama. He needed to feel her loving warmth, for her to place her hands on either side of his face as she kissed his forehead and tucked him back into bed, saving him from his foolish fears. He took a deep breath and crept down, each stair creaking as he went.

The ground floor of their little house was just one long room. The walls were crowded with shelves upon shelves of pots and pans. Murky jars of medicinal-smelling ointments lined every cabinet. Benji didn't know what most of them were, but he knew that they stung like crazy when they were slicked onto the perpetual tide of cuts and bruises that young boys collect like frogspawn.

Most of the far wall was taken up by a fireplace, empty, and a large cooking pot that still held some cold remains of their evening stew.

However, the main thing, the most awful thing about the room, was that his Mama was not there.

He thought about running to Amanda. She stayed in one of the houses on the other side of the village now. But if he went to Amanda and told her that Mama had left him alone, she would be angry. She would shout at Mama again, like she had before, and it would be bad. Benji hated it when they argued.

He could go to Margaret, he supposed, but as soon as this thought popped into his head, he knew that he never would.

Margaret could be mean, especially if he went and woke her up in the middle of the night. Amanda said that Margaret was a fear-monger and a busybody. Once, when he and Amanda had been sorting the clothing and Amanda had thought that they were alone, she had called Margaret an *old hag*. Benji didn't really know what that meant, but they had both squealed with laughter anyway. Mama had heard them and had called Amanda wicked for saying such things. His sister had been angry and said that she had a right to her own opinion, and they had another of their arguments. He had pleaded with Amanda to say that she was sorry, but she hadn't.

No. The best thing by far would be for him to find Mama by himself. It was the brave thing to do. It's what the hunters would do.

He straightened his back and marched with more confidence than he felt to the front door.

The door was tall, and the latch was high. He had to stand on tiptoe to reach and even then, could only brush at it with his fingertips. It took a few moments and one ungainly hop for him to finally be able to unlatch it. He tried not to think about monsters. He tried not to think about being snatched.

The door swung inwards.

After a few moments, when no monsters rushed into the room snapping their teeth, rotten breath gagging, ready to tear the flesh from his bones, he peeped out into the night.

The sky was clear, and he could see a fingernail-sliver of moon just starting to rise from behind the row of houses. A flour-dusting of stars filled the rest of the night sky.

He held onto the door tightly, ready to slam it at the slightest evidence of monster. He leaned out over the doorstep. A quick glance told him that the houses around him, stone-built and clustered tightly against the earth-packed road, were silent. A little further away the village square was visible only as darkness against darkness. The air was warm and fragrant with the flowery sweetness of a dying summer. Somewhere overhead he heard the hoot of an owl, a soft sound that was swiftly followed by a high-pitched shriek as some furry creature died a squealing death.

He swallowed.

Maybe it wasn't such a good idea for him to go out looking for his Mama. After all, she always said that if ever he was in trouble he should go to the house and wait for her there. She might even be angry at him if he wandered the village in the dark. In fact, he knew that she would be.

He was ready to go back inside again, to close the door against the darkness and wait for her to come home, when he noticed someone in the distance. They had their back to him and were walking towards the silhouette of the church that sat just beyond the square at the end of the road. Even so, he instantly recognised the whiteness of her cardigan that reached almost to her knees, and her pale hair that seemed to glow in the moonlight.

'Mama,' he whisper-shouted, standing on tiptoes and waving his arm in the air. 'Mama, wait!'

Maybe Benji wasn't loud enough, or maybe she was simply too far away – either way, she didn't hear him. She disappeared around the corner. Benji teetered on the step for a moment, a war going on within his small body between his fear of the monsters that lurked in the dark, and his unwavering love for his Mama.

Finally, love won over fear. He ran inside and grabbed the poker that sat in the empty fireplace. Now that he was armed, he felt braver. He ran into the night, shoeless.

Benji trotted down the row of houses, staying within the moonshine and purposefully away from the shadows. He gripped the poker so tightly that it hurt his hand. He could hear occasional soft snores coming from the houses that he passed, even though their doors and windows were all tightly bolted.

He had never been out in the nighttime by himself before, and the stillness and quietness of the dark unnerved him. Normally, his days were filled with people, chores and snorting animals. Farmyard smells and hands wrinkled into pale, fleshy gloves from spending too much time submerged in the washing vats. It was curious to be alone now. He wasn't sure that he liked it too much, he wasn't sure he liked how darkness and fear could keep everyone hidden away inside.

He imagined what would happen if anyone looked out of their window and saw him walking down the street in the middle of the night, in his pajamas, without any shoes, armed with a poker. They would probably rush out to demand to know what he was doing, angry at first but then when he explained that his Mama was gone, that she might need help, they would be grateful. They would admire how brave he was, putting his Mama's needs first and risking the nighttime to help her. They would walk with him, at first just a few but then many, and they would arrive together in the square. His Mama would be there, grateful for his help and for saving her from her mysterious nighttime wanderings. The noise from the crowd would draw more attention, and the hunters would come out of their lodge. They would see how brave and strong he was and would beg him to join them. Amanda would be there too, happy and tearful with pride.

Practically skipping now, he arrived in the square. But there were no admiring followers, no proud hunters ready to welcome him into their ranks, and his Mama was not there.

Before him was the village square. To the left the church loomed above, its spire blocking out the light from the stars. A hunt had returned just a few days earlier and the square was still littered with flower garlands and petals. So bright in daytime, the night had leached them of all colour, making them seem droopingly dull. The watch-fire had burned down to glowing embers and sent a single plume of smoke up to the stars.

Beyond that, on the other side of the square, was the gate. It was huge. To Benji it felt like it must be over one hundred feet tall, although Amanda said it was nowhere near that. It had an intricate painting of a pair of antlers, entwined with flowers and birds. It was the symbol of the hunters, the emblem of their goodness and purity. It was beautiful. The only times the gates were ever opened were on hunt days. Otherwise, they were tightly locked for everybody's safety.

Except for now.

Benji felt a rush of panic, his guts twisting.

The gate was open.

He shrank against the wall, his terror now a physical thing that pressed his chest so hard that he couldn't breathe. He didn't want to look. But a small, defiant part of him wanted to look more than anything.

It was forbidden for anyone to open the gates. Only the hunters could give permission, and they never did. Benji couldn't think of any reason why anyone would want to open them anyway. He had only ever seen them opened a handful of times, and even then, it was at a safe distance, peering out from behind his Mama's skirt.

The punishment for opening the gate without permission was bad.

He whimpered, the sound echoing around the square, and squeezed his eyes shut. He ran blindly, his hand trailing along the wall for guidance. He ran towards the hunter's lodge, as that was the only safe place he could think of.

He had nearly reached it, nearly reached safety, when his foot hit something and he tripped. He sprawled forwards and fell with his hands out, painfully tearing the skin on his palms and knees. He landed in something wet and warm. He scrabbled around and the sight before him chased any fears of monsters and open gates straight out of his head. He let out a low moan.

'Mama, mama, mama.' He sobbed, pulling at the cardigan that he had watched his Mama make every evening, and which she wore now. It was white no longer. She was lying with her back to him, and there was something terrifying in the still way that she was slumped on the ground.

He pulled at her. She rolled in a boneless kind of way towards him. There was so much blood. He tried scooping it back towards her, as if he could push it back inside, but soon stopped. With a trembling hand, he brushed a few strands of her pale hair from her forehead, but moaned in misery when he only succeeded in smearing blood across her face. She stared past him, towards the moon.

Fat tears slipped down his cheeks and pattered onto the ground. He shook her once and then twice, kneeling in the sticky mess and using his whole body in his effort to move her.

'Don't go, Mama,' he begged, burying his face into her hair. 'Please don't go. Don't go without me.'

She didn't respond; she just stared past him.

He tucked himself in close to his Mama, delving his hands into her cardigan to soak up her rapidly dwindling warmth.

There he stayed, crying, trembling, refusing to believe what his eyes were telling him. His Mama would not leave him. Not ever.

But before too long he became aware of a strange noise, a soft scraping. He looked up, breath hiccoughing in his chest. For what seemed like a lifetime, the moment stayed frozen, the small boy cradling his Mama's body, with the creature standing before him. But then in a rush he screamed, throwing himself backwards and away.

Benji ran, his small bloody footprints disappearing into the dark, with the monster following closely behind.

CHAPTER TWO – AMANDA

'Down in the valley, where the green grass grows, there sat Benji, sweet as a rose. Along came a monster, who ate him up for tea, you might've caught him, but you can't catch me! 1,2,3,4...'

The girls chanted in unison, skipping to the beat of their song. Their rope arced through the air as they hopped in and out, bare feet kicking up clouds of dust, frayed rope thumping as it swung downwards. Sometimes they darted glances at Amanda, sitting on the steps of the church nearby.

The song hurt, Amanda couldn't deny that, but it wasn't the first time that she had heard it, and it wasn't the worst. The girls never acknowledged Amanda as they sang, but she knew that they watched her. They waited for a reaction. Amanda found some satisfaction in not giving it to them.

They were too smart to make it obvious, of course. Instead, along with the glances, they sent little nods and whispers in her direction. Amanda still ignored it. But inevitably the whispers would get louder, and then there would be giggles. At this point, Amanda would look up and the girls would pretend that they had not done anything, would continue skipping and singing, for all the world as if they had not noticed Amanda at all.

It always went like this. Every morning, for the last year and a half. They knew that Amanda could not admonish them; it was not her place. These girls were children of the hunters. The official children. And Amanda was not.

So the girls whispered and giggled, never too loudly, and Amanda pretended that she didn't hear them.

Being too old for school, yet not quite of age, meant that Amanda was often given the task of watching the younger children before school started. She didn't mind it so much, particularly on mornings like this one. The sun had just risen above the steeple of the church and light filled the square. It reflected off the dust that was kicked up by the girls' feet and seemed to make the air sparkle and shimmer. A pair of swifts flitted around above her head, buzzing trills and descending scales, and one fat wood pigeon sat in a crevice in the church steeple, cooing. A small breeze brought with it scents of baking bread and wildflowers, filling Amanda with a contentedness that she had not felt in a long time.

Bored with their game, the girls had stopped skipping and were gathered around

Mara, the oldest of the group. She had brought something out of her pocket and was showing it to the others.

'What is it?' one of the girls asked in a whisper.

'My Da brought it back from his last hunt. He says it's very special, just like me.' Mara said with a smile and a slight flush in her cheeks. 'It's probably the only one left in the world.'

The girls gathered closer. Amanda couldn't see what Mara had, but it was small enough to fit in the palm of her hand. One of the girls reached out to touch it, but Mara snatched it away, closing her hand over it in a fist.

'Look with your eyes not your hands,' she said through her teeth.

The school bell rang, echoing across the square, and the girls immediately turned around. They wiggled back into their shoes, then ran, skipped, and hopped towards the building that was used as the girls' schoolhouse. Mara walked more slowly than the others, putting whatever she had carefully back in her pocket. Amanda saw a flash of colour, something impossibly blue and pink, but nothing more. Mara kept her eyes lowered as she passed close, but she flicked her long hair in Amanda's direction.

The girls made a weaving, bobbing line in front of their teacher. Others joined them, the unofficial children walking to the back of the line. Next door was the boys' school. A row of boys of very mixed ages were lining up, fewer of them than the girls. They were scuffing their shoes in the dust and playfully shoving each other when their teacher wasn't looking.

Amanda tried not to watch them, but her eyes kept on drifting back as if of their own accord. There was one boy who was standing with his back to her. Amanda guessed that he was around eight, given his size, though he could have been older. He had dark hair, the ends curled around his collar. His ears stuck out slightly, and he was scuffing his shoe in the dust. Amanda's heart jumped a little in her chest. Even though she knew better. Even though every time she did this it hurt just as much as the day that she was told about what happened. She couldn't help it. And of course, the boy turned around, and it was not him. It was some other boy with wavy hair and sticking out ears. And her heart broke all over again.

Amanda walked away from the square. She had more chores to do, of course. The one thing that you could rely on was chores - they were always there for you. But right now she wanted nothing more than to be away from the children. Away from the square. Maybe even away from the village.

Although, no, never that.

She drifted along the high street, away from the church, and past the lodge. She was used to being alone, now more than ever, but that didn't make it any easier. The funny thing was that when she was alone, she craved companionship, but when she was with others, she longed to be alone. There was no winning.

She found herself outside the kitchens. The doors were propped open, and steam and heat billowed out. Inside shadowy figures moved around in a white haze. Margaret was standing near the door pounding dough over and over. Her arms were coated with flour up to the elbow, and a tray of already baked loaves wafted steam on a table next to her.

Margaret was known throughout the village to be a force of nature – impatient, aggressive, and self-possessed. She had been born without hair, and kept her head wrapped tightly in a black scarf. She drew her eyebrows in every day with charcoal – thick, ashy arches that made her seem permanently disapproving. She was a large woman, in height as well as girth. Amanda often wondered, if Margaret's hairlessness had been obvious at birth, whether she would have been culled. But that had been decades before Amanda had been born, and she would never dare ask that out loud. Not within Margaret's earshot anyway.

Margaret was looking at her with her eyes narrowed and ashy brows puckered. A bead of sweat dribbled down the side of her face and fell onto the dough she was pounding.

'Don't tell me you ain't got jobs to do,' Margaret said, shaking her red and sweaty face. 'Don't tell me that, not today. Hunters save me, does anyone else in this village have a smidgen of common sense? I'm too busy to find jobs for idle hands, so don't ask me.'

She was in one of her moods. Again. Amanda didn't have the energy for an argument today and didn't want to set the older woman off.

'I wasn't going to ask you,' Amanda said. 'I'm here for the scraps. I'll take them up to the pens.'

Margaret huffed, but didn't argue, which must have been a first. Maybe her mood wasn't all that bad after all. She nodded into the depths of the steam-filled kitchen.

'Ain't much to give these days. Slops're over by the back wall, for what they're worth.'

Amanda hesitated. She hated it in the kitchens and didn't want to go into that hot and sticky room, so full of sweating bodies. But she had told Margaret that she would do it now, and if she didn't the older woman might find her something worse to do. She would probably send her to the latrines out of spite.

Amanda braced herself before entering the chaos. Men and women ran around, carrying trays of steaming food, bags of vegetables, and stacks of wooden bowls. Breakfast had long since finished and they were now busily preparing lunch. A couple of girls similar to her own age were bottling fruit in the corner, ready for the winter stores. That used to be Amanda's job, but since the break-in most people seemed too scared to ask her to do things. Like they might get tainted by tragedy. Like it might be catching. Most couldn't even meet her eyes.

The centre of the room was taken up with a large firepit that was rarely put out, dominated by a pot so large that Amanda could climb into it if she'd wanted to. Now it was bubbling with a thickly glutenous porridge that was standard fare on hunt days. The meals were simpler when the hunters were not in residence, usually made up of porridge and vegetables. Or vegetables and porridge.

Amanda spied the scraps bucket against the far wall and hurried across the room, narrowly avoiding a swipe from a ladle wielded by a frowning George when she dared to get too close to the fire.

She grabbed the bucket and hurried out again, glad to be in the relative coolness of the summer's morning. She peered in; Margaret was right, there wasn't much. Some carrot peelings, husks of cabbages, and some potatoes that were far too rotten.

Margaret was leaning against the wall of the kitchen now, seemingly taking a break. She was staring up at the church steeple.

'They've been gone for nearly a week now, that's too long,' she said with a shaking of her head. 'I pray every day that the hunt'll return with good tidings. And fresh food.'

There was nothing for Amanda to say. She prayed for the same thing, but she didn't want to talk about it – she was already tired of Margaret and longed to be by herself. She turned away from the heat and the busy shouts from inside the kitchens.

'Mind you don't take all day!' Magaret shouted at her back as she walked away alone up the lane.

CHAPTER THREE – BENJI

When he had been younger, once school had finished and his chores were done and Mama agreed that his time was his own, Benji would beg Amanda to go with him to see the goats. He loved their earth-smelling fur and strange eyes, ready to nibble on anything that came close enough, even his fingers if he wasn't careful. Amanda would tut and huff and say that she was too busy, but he knew that if he wheedled enough, she would eventually give in.

Sometimes, if Benji was lucky, Olivia, Amanda's friend, would come too. Benji loved it when that happened, even though it was rare, and he would follow both girls excitably as they talked to one another, running in zigzags across their path, getting under their feet and bringing them interesting stones that he found along the way.

On this particular day it was cold, and as they left the house, they had all wrapped themselves up in woollen blankets secured with belts, as well as thick hats and gloves. He was wearing at least three pairs of socks inside his boots, and his feet felt uncomfortably squeezed. He ran down the street ahead of Amanda and Olivia and jumped into a puddle. However, it was frozen solid, and he didn't even make a crack. Instead, his heels skidded on the frozen ground, and he nearly fell over backwards.

Together, they trotted up the street and its closely packed houses, crossed over the square, and walked past the church and the hunters' lodge.

Olivia sped up, her arms wrapped tightly around herself with Amanda hurrying behind her. Benji called to them to slow down but Amanda had said *'Hush and mind your own business!'*

Benji slowed down as they walked past the lodge. Normally at least one hunter would be around and would wave at him through the windows, sometimes giving him a little salute. Today they were all out on a hunt so there was no one there other than Margaret doing the cleaning and she never waved.

He had never been inside the building because he was not a hunter and was not old enough to do chores for them, but he had heard lots of stories from the older boys about the treasures that were inside. Probably the most precious, kept in special cupboards to protect them from time and moths, was the armour that had been made in the olden times. Once, his friend Mike who was a few years older than him told him that he had actually touched the armour, though Benji didn't believe him. Mike was a liar. They were light as air, he said, but could repel any knife or dagger that was thrust at them. Mama said that this was because they were made of special fabric that only the olden people knew how to make, but Benji was certain that it must be some kind of magic that was weaved into the stitching. Only the hunters could wear them, and only on hunting days. Benji wished he could have one, and he wrapped his blanket even tighter around himself, imagining that it was monster-proof armour. He picked up a stick and stabbed and thrusted at imaginary foes.

DENISE BENNETT

Denise Bennett is a doctor who has worked in hospital and general practice. Her first novel, a retelling of *Titus Andronicus*, melds her love of Shakespeare's tragic plays and crime fiction. She lives near Guildford with her husband, son, a dog and two cats.

denisebennett@me.com

The Ravenous Tiger

An extract from the midpoint of a novel

The novel is a retelling of Shakespeare's revenge tragedy, *Titus Andronicus*, and is set in London in the near future (2032). Here is a thumbnail sketch of the events which lead up to the extract.

Tina Andrews, aged thirty-eight, is a highly-ranked detective at London City Central Police who has recently been suspended while investigating the murder of a prominent businesswoman's son. Tina's twin children, Quin and Lavinia, seventeen, and Ben, Lavinia's boyfriend, have been attacked while helping out at a dog rescue centre by the Thames in west London. The attackers murdered Ben, drugged Quin and dumped both of them into the cellar of a derelict house.

Quin is now in hospital and about to be erroneously charged with murder, while Lavinia is missing. The investigations into Ben's murder and Lavinia's disappearance are being supervised by a hostile detective from West London Police, who has warned a distraught Tina to stay away.

The extract begins the day after the attack when Tina, supported by her junior officer, DC Rana, attempts to access the crime scene.

***

THE RIVER
London, October 2032

The elevated section of the A40 which led to London's western suburbs had been shut to all but priority vehicles since April 1, 2028. The closure caused mayhem in the surrounding roads, but today Tina offered a secular prayer of thanks as Rana drove their squad car at speed towards the turnpike, its lights signalling green.

The city was a multilayered beast. From here on the raised highway, she could see three, no four, fires which burned in the streets below despite the on-off rain. Visibility remained poor as lazy curls of smoke drifted into the drizzle. The overhead gantries flashed blurred rotations of neon-yellow messages: *President DeSantis's State Visit ENN tonight! ... Be Road Safe 17 fatalities today! ... Home Secretary Announces Crime Package No. 3! ... Renew your biometric ID now! ... Capital Punishment Referendum 10 days 18 hrs 35 mins.*

'Capital punishment, ma'am? You think it'll happen?' said Rana.

'Doubt it.' She glanced at Rana who usually went bareheaded, but today wore a lilac-coloured hijab which didn't completely hide the red-purplish bruising to the left side of her face. 'You OK?'

'Yes, ma'am,' said Rana, her eyes fixed on the road ahead.

They were out of *Priority Vehicles Only* now and the traffic had slowed to stationary; an ambulance behind bleated a forlorn, impotent wail in its attempt to cut through. Trouble lay ahead. A beefy, bald man leapt out of a lorry two vehicles in front. Eyes bulging, fists balled, he thumped on the passenger window of the car adjacent, spewing ugly-faced obscenities. Horns blared. He gave a vigorous middle finger salute to the world in general before unzipping his flies, urinating first on the car beside him and then in the direction of the hooting vehicles.

Tina opened her door wide so that the police logo could be seen. 'Oi!' she yelled, leaning out, 'Police. Move!'

With a final, sneery flip of the bird at her, he climbed back into his lorry.

Soon after, they took a left off the Great West Rd. Two fire-blackened shells of cars in a V formation blocked their path. A huddle of lads, mid-teens, sat on the pavement, watching them approach. One stood and gestured, 'Bring it on,' with a curl of his hands.

'Turn around,' Tina said.

'It's one way, ma'am.'

'Turn around. Do it.'

She could hear the cheers of the boys as Rana executed a three-point turn; they both ducked reflexively at the sharp clunks of cans and stones which hit the back of the car.

'Will I be in trouble? Like, if there's any dents?'

'No. Go on, there's a gap.'

Rana drove back onto the main road, ignoring the honking of other drivers, and tried the next left.

'There, see The Griffin Brewery? Pull in behind,' said Tina.

'Not much of it now, is there?'

'No.'

Only the high roadside wall that ran to the river appeared intact. Most of the back of the building had collapsed, the foundations repeatedly undermined by flooding and subsidence. The graffiti *London Pride Forever!* in red spray paint failed to cheer the dismal regulation blue of government security panels which cloaked this end of the ruin. She could just make out the fabled Griffin icon still clinging to the side wall, a hint of gold showing through its blackened body.

'Time to set up your bit of kit,' said Tina.

Rana retrieved the device from her jacket's pocket and fiddled with it. 'S'all ready, ma'am.'

'Let's walk down and try it out. There's the sentry vehicles.' She nodded towards two police cars that straddled the road running to the river, about seventy or so metres away.

The once chi-chi street looked careworn and crumbling. Sad elegant houses had gone to seed, with pale grey brickwork stained dark in places and mottled with algae. Metal grilles protected doors and ground-floor windows from intruders; boards covered most upper windows and the remainder were broken. Acid-yellow notices pockmarked the walls, boasting ownership by the Rivermead Developments Co. which had bought for knockdown prices during the death spiral of the house price collapse. But the company had overextended, and the promised redevelopment had yet to arrive. This area would soon join the Condemned List, Tina thought. A jaundiced woman sat on the pavement amongst a detritus of carrier bags, her back against a garden fence, breastfeeding her baby. She watched them with disinterested eyes as they passed.

'Who's Peter Chapman?' said Rana.

Tina followed the direction of Rana's gaze. An urban artwork of a man in a hangman's noose stood life size on the brewery wall, head angled sharply from his body, face contorted, purple tongue hanging out through a grotesque smile. Letters scrawled beneath read *RIH Peter Chapman, - Activist E521 for Action for Housing.*

'RIH... Rot in Hell,' said Tina. 'And Chapman's a slumlord. Ran Rivermead, see those signs? In prison now. His flunkies beat up an old couple who wouldn't sell up, and the man died. But there's fifty more greedy bastards lording it all around London now.'

'So who owns all this?'

Tina shrugged. 'Some government department, I guess. Chapman's assets were confiscated by the state.'

'What's—'

'Shh. Activate the blocker now.'

A police officer had emerged from the first squad car and stood there, resting his arm on its open door, watching them approach. His small, piggy eyes looked lost in his puffy face.

Rana fiddled with the device and pocketed it. 'Done,' she said.

'Is it working?'

She nodded, and smiled up at Tina, like a child waiting for approval.

'Stick to the script.'

'I'm DC Rana,' she said to the officer. 'I'm on a training assessment day. Um... this is my supervisor, DCSu Tina An...' Rana let her voice trail away into a mumble,

'You got clearance?' he said.

'Yes, sir.'

He muttered something and ducked his head into the car, pulling out the e-identifier.

'Put your prints here.' He indicated the touch panel.

Rana complied.

The identifier emitted a shrill beep. The policeman glared at the device, switching it off and then back on again. The screen remained black and the beeping resumed.

'Sodding tech,' he said.

'Would this help?' Rana showed her ID.

He squinted at it. 'City Central? You're a long way out.'

'Yeah, that's what I said when I got given this assignment,' she said, her eyes wide with innocence. 'Guess I've got to go where I'm sent though.'

'Or else they'll thump you, right?' He laughed and pointed a pudgy finger at Rana's face.

Her hand flew to the bruising on her face and she pulled the scarf forward. 'Yes, sir, they might,' she said, riding the joke, but her body stiffened with evident embarrassment. 'I mean, you could call City Central and check if you want,' she continued, her tone nothing but agreeable. 'The organiser is Marcus.'

He emitted theatrical sighs as he scrolled and prodded his handset.

C'mon Marcus, please pick up, thought Tina.

The officer spoke briefly into his device, staring ahead at nothing in particular, then gave them the side-eye and nodded.

'Alright, you're in,' he said to Rana, handing her back her ID.

Tina held out her identification card, but he barely glanced at it.

'There are two officers down there,' he said. 'I'll let them know you're on the way. Not that there's anything to see now. Heard forensics've got what they need. Everyone must be out in forty minutes, before the super-high tide. Hope you've got your wellies,' he added, with a snigger.

Once out of earshot, Rana whispered, 'He's an idiot, ma'am. Does it look like we've got our wellies?'

'No. He's an idiot,' she agreed. 'But you did well.'

*

The rain had eased, allowing a faint sphere of sun to peep through the grey cloud cover. It cast a solemn, mournful light on the stretch of the Thames which opened out ahead of them. The waters spilled across the bank-side gardens, and into the road where they stood; an insolent rebuke to the 'Severe Flooding' sign atop a post which leaned thirty or so degrees out of true. Most of the broken wall which divided the river from the roadway of the Mall looked as though it had been eaten away by a giant mouth. Beyond that, grew reeds and bushes: presumably what was left of the once-tended gardens that adorned the riverside path. They partially obscured a full view of the river. Through a gap, Tina could see a specialist boat with a police blue-yellow logo unloading their gear. Above it circled a bird of prey. A wetsuited diver leaned over the edge, peering down at something that had caught his interest. She watched him dangle his hand into the water and it felt as if his cold fingers had reached into her chest, squeezing icily around her heart, preventing it from beating.

A gentle hand on her arm. 'Ma'am? Ma'am?...'

She looked down at Rana, compassion written on the younger woman's face.

'Can't do nothing about that, ma'am. We could search along here though, yeah?'

Tina nodded.

A duck paddled by on the flooded road, but the illusion of pastoral serenity was undermined by a patch of bubbles which broke the surface, from a drain perhaps, or something worse.

'Look at that, ma'am! Could there be...y'know something decomposing like—'

'It's not deep enough here to conceal a body,' she said, but her throat tightened nonetheless. She took her shoes off and handed them to Rana, rolled up her jeans, and waded into the cold water, feeling rough cracks in the hard ground beneath the soles of her feet. The duck waggled its tail feathers in irritation at her approach and glided away as she crouched down and reached through the bubbles, her fingers exploring, hitting smooth metal. The unmistakable whiff of sewage burned her nostrils. Nothing but a drain.

She wanted a proper view of the river. Ignoring the seeping wetness, she climbed over the wall at its lowest until she got a clear sight of Chiswick Eyot. The long island stretched several hundred metres parallel to the bank, dividing the Thames into a narrow channel on this side, and a wider one on the other. The island itself was submerged now, at high tide, but the crowns of weeping willow trees rose proudly, before drooping down into the water, a few yellowed leaves clinging on to the trailing stems. A helicopter whirred above, sending hundreds of acid-green parakeets screeching into the air, flapping and diving low over her head before they resettled squawking in the trees. Two black-clad figures waded waist deep in the channel about thirty metres downstream to her right; four or five more busied themselves close to the bank further upstream. Police divers. The rushing in her ears warned her to bend forward, head down, hands on her thighs. Breathe in, one, two, three, four. Breathe out, one, two, three, four, five, six. Slow it down. Slow it down. Look at the water here. A fly rode upon a pale willow leaf that floated by. It poked the leaf with its proboscis, jumped around a few times and then took off. Another one landed. The leaf drifted away, downstream. Her breathing felt... more in control. If the divers were still searching, she reasoned, they hadn't found Lavinia.

She put her fear into a mental box, and straightened up, slow and steady, pulling her phone camera from her pocket. The divers clustered near two bankside boats to the east, and one to the west; yellow and blue-striped river patrols guarded the mid-stream access to the area. A red speedboat motored by, out of range of the exclusion zone, slowing right down until it mostly disappeared from view behind the island. Her eyes tracked it, catching glimpses between the drooping branches of the willows. It appeared to have stopped, then about-turned in an illegal move, crawling back the way it had come. A persistent gawper, most likely, but she set the camera to max magnification and snapped.

The kestrel had returned, unbothered by the receding noise of the chopper, hovering directly above her in an elegant smear of rust-red against the grey sky. It had seen its lunch, she thought, scanning the reeds close by. There. An object broke the water's surface, stuck in the vegetation. Too small to be human, she told herself.

It's not Lavinia. It'll be a fox or a bag of rubbish or... she stumbled and stepped on something sharp, falling to her knees, one hand down in the water. Reaching out towards the object with her free hand, she felt wet fur. Fur. Not human.

Her eyes prickled with relief. She lifted the animal a little. A lifeless, sand-coloured dog, maybe fifteen kilos, not decomposed at all. Floppy. No rigor mortis. She didn't know the rigor period for dogs, but she guessed that it had died within the last twenty-four hours. A small round wound on its flank looked like a gunshot. Quin had said something about a dog that had been shot just before the attackers came in. Maybe this was the one.

She carried it back to where Rana waited on the pavement.

'Oh, poor little thing. But, ma'am, I think it's dead.'

'Good detective skills. Let's bag him up.'

Rana rummaged in her backpack and found one large enough. 'You think it's a clue?'

Tina shrugged. 'Maybe. Hold it open so I can get him in.'

She manoeuvered the dog into the bag and set it down behind a withering buddleia that straggled from between broken flagstones, then secured the two drawstrings around a thick basal branch. She broke a couple of stems from the bush and laid them across the bag so that the dead brown blossoms rendered it barely visible to a casual observer.

'Aaw, flowers on the grave, like,' murmured Rana.

Tina bit back a sarcastic response and put her socks and boots back on, wincing a little. The sole of her foot still bled and left a few red splotches on the damp ground, its wetness shaping the blood spots into faint laciness. She squinted against a flitting ray of sunlight, looking eastwards up the Mall. A series of orange bollards and a uniformed officer guarded a white house.

'That's where the action is,' she said. 'Come on.'

*

The houses facing the river were in a more advanced state of disrepair than those in the side streets, with a waist-high tide mark of black and green mould patches rising on the external walls. The police officer at the scene perched on a fold-up chair, legs crossed, wiggling in her seat. She caught sight of them as they approached and stopped moving.

'Detectives Rana and er... Tina An...?'

'Yes,' said Tina.

'I'm PC Baines. You're just taking a look, yeah, ma'am?'

'And a few photos.' She glanced at the house. 'Doesn't look like the Secure-It team's been in yet?'

'No. That's just a temporary patch-up job.'

'Mmm. You been stuck here all morning?'

'Since six a.m.,' Baines said, her face pinched.

Tina shook her head. 'You're entitled to a comfort break.'

Baines nodded. A forlorn, blonde curl quivered on her forehead.

'There must be a toilet at the vet centre. Just round that corner, isn't it?' said Tina, pointing to the street sign that read 'Eyot Green.'

'Yes, ma'am.'

'You go then,' said Tina. 'We'll watch the shop.'

'You sure?' Relief chased away the doubt on Baines's face. 'You won't tell anyone?'

'Not a soul.'

'Five minutes max, I promise!' She hurried away, using short careful steps, shouting over her shoulder, 'Please don't go past the barriers!'

THE CELLAR

Once Baines was out of sight, Tina went past the barriers. They ran the width of a double-fronted, Georgian house with a small front garden bounded by a low, lichen-blotched stone wall. Tall metal poles rose vertically just behind; previously supports for hi-spec glass or perspex panels to protect against intruders, they now held stretches of a wire security fence. A whole section had been removed centrally, presumably by the first responders. Towards the left, on the boundary with next door, she could see a gap where an overgrown elder tree had pushed out of the garden, breaking the wall down to a mere few inches in height and distorting the fencing. It looked like the gap had been extended by a couple of feet, making a space too insignificant for standard police crime-scene access. But the clean edges of the wire told her that someone had cut into that fence recently. She called out to Rana and told her to stay outside and watch out for Baines's return. Putting on a pair of gloves, she climbed through, taking care not to snag herself on the sharp, protruding ends.

The ground rustled, the flick of a rat's tail sending mounds of autumn leaves into a mini flurry. Grasses and weeds appeared to be flattened in an indistinct path leading to the house. Foot traffic or a body dragged through? Or just the forensic teams? No signs of blood spill, but the rain would've washed that away. Picking her way through, she ducked to avoid the overarching stem of a thorny wild rose, but it seemed to reach for her, tugging her hair, scratching her face, almost poking into her right eye. As she cursed and sought to disentangle herself, a tiny blue flower smiled prettily amongst the blood-red hips and withered leaves. Only it wasn't a flower. It was a sliver of fabric, caught on a savage thorn. She plucked it off and slipped it into an evidence bag in her inside jacket pocket.

Up close, the white house was not that white. Vines, mostly bare save for a few crimson leaves, had rooted their tendrils into the surface render, exposing patches of dull, red brick beneath. Glassless windows sported rotten-looking wooden frames behind the guards of their metal bars. Although the symmetrical façade boasted an impressive portico, raised by six stone steps, the lintel plasterwork had crumbled and a Victorian lamp dangled at a crazy angle from a loose, exposed cable. Plastic sheeting covered the doorway, tacked by strips of crime scene tape.

Tina peeled off a strip of tape and edged into the hallway of the house. The front door, detached from its frame, rested against the wall to the left. The hinges had gone completely, their site marked by pale, fresh splinterings. She flashed her torch. Spots of black mould grew on dingy yellowing walls but an internal tidemark appeared to be absent - presumably, the stone steps elevated the entrance hall above the floodlines. The dank air reeked of decay, dead mice and rats maybe, or something worse.

A corridor ahead led to reception rooms, but the strips of tape across a narrow wooden door, immediately to the right, pointed to the investigation hot spot. She picked the tape off the door and pulled it open, recoiling from the black space of a hole. A cellar, she realised. But the steps inside it were to the side and too low to access from where she stood. Puzzled, she flashed her torch, catching the glint of a metal ring on the floor, like an evil eye peering up at her.

It was the handle of a trap door.

She grasped it and tugged; a cold sweat prickled at the back of her neck. With a grunt of effort, the trap jolted up and revealed a connecting set of wooden steps. She photographed the access to the cellar and made her way down.

Empty wine racks spanning three walls remained surprisingly well-preserved; although the cellar was below the waterline, it was protected from flooding by its stone construction and the elevation of the ground floor. She took more photos, keeping her phone camera in torch mode while she looked around. Those rust-brown stains near her feet - blood, most likely. She shivered. Was Ben still alive when he'd been thrown down here? Quin would have been in pain, frightened... she shook her head, banishing those thoughts, and focused on photographing everything she saw. The stains, the racks, the stack of cardboard boxes in the far corner and two pictures which were propped against them.

Something about the pictures drew her in. They were clear of dust, unlike the boxes against which they rested. The smaller painting depicted a black wildcat - a panther - on a red background, fangs gleaming yellow in its open mouth, poised and ready to leap. The other sported an elaborate border of fabric roses woven with rusty barbed wire, which surrounded a hyper-real portrait of a young woman in a white dress. Red ribbons erupted from between her lips; she held her arms aloft and more ribbons fell from where her hands should have been, curling long and pretty onto the dirty floor.

Her phone vibrated and she jumped. 'Rana?'

'PC Baines is coming back.'

She took some final photos before she sped up the steps, dropped the trapdoor and closed up the cellar access, doing her best to re-stick the tape across the door. Back in the garden, she squeezed between the elder tree and the fence, so that she was leaning against the barrier gulping fresh air as Baines rounded the corner with Rana.

'Thanks, ma'am,' said PC Baines. 'If you want to check out the vet centre you've only got a few minutes before they lock up so... There's a PC down there and the vet, euthanising the animals.'

'Euthanising them?' said Rana, 'Why?'

Baines shrugged, 'Mine's not to reason why, detectives.'

*

They turned into Eyot Green, a narrow road that ran off The Mall. The jaunty outline of a dog had been spray painted on the side wall of the corner house in bright fuchsia, alongside the words 'Veterinary Urgent Care'. Properties to the side and ahead sported the familiar sight of barred windows and doors, but the tatty yellow Rivermead Development notices had been mostly torn down and replaced by vibrant paintings of pink paw prints.

A squad car ahead flashed its lights at them. As they drew close, the passenger side window slid down to the accompaniment of a tinny radio ballad; a hand emerged and lazily waved them on.

Tina gave them a thumbs up. Sloppy bastards, she thought.

The little road had widened into a blind tarmacked area, at the back of which ran standard state-issued corrugated fence topped with wire spikes. The signage warned: 'Keep Out! Under Local Government Condemnation Review'. A grey Portakabin enlivened by a painting of a black cat with huge green eyes occupied about a quarter of the space; a vet's vehicle was parked in front.

'Check out the perimeter,' she said to Rana. 'Look for any sites of access, or where that fence has been breached.'

'Yes, ma'am.'

'Photograph everything.'

'I will.' She hurried off.

A tall, brawny man in green scrubs emerged from the mobile building carrying an inert dog, its legs dangling. He put it carefully into the back of a white van marked 'West London Veterinary Services', closing over the doors as she approached, but not before she'd seen a jumble of fur inside.

'Excuse me, my name's Tina Andrews. Can I have a word?'

He turned to her, his unshaven jaw set tight.

'My son Quin helped out here. He was attacked last night. He's in hospital and his sister – my daughter – is missing.'

'Andrews...? A flitter of recognition lit his eyes. 'Quin's mother?'

'Yes. You know him?'

'He's my student. I'm Baz Turner. Did you know he'd been sleeping here?'

She bridled at his aggressive tone. 'He said you'd be here. And security. I'd never have agreed—'

He snorted. 'We don't have the resources for a security guard. Or overnight cover for veterinary staff. I'd applied for it, but after this...' He shook his head.

'So, at night—'

'We give the animals their drugs and fluids. Lock up, come back the next morning.' He pointed at the centre, then jabbed a finger towards her. 'That's what Quin should've done. But instead, he was using and dealing.'

'Whoa, that's not—'

'Look, I've not got time for this.' He tried to push past her, but she held her ground.

'No, *you* look. You're wrong,' she said, squaring up to him. 'He was attacked here last night while caring for these animals - unpaid, a young volunteer at *your* project with no security. I mean, no security, for fuck's sake? Now he's in hospital, terrified, with police at the end of his bed and his sister - my daughter - is missing.' Her voice had risen in pitch to a crescendo which broke over the final few words.

The vet's eyes searched her face, his gaze less hard now. 'OK. I'm sorry. But I don't see what I can do. And I've got three more dogs to euthanise.'

She passed the back of her hand across her eyes, brushing away the wetness that threatened. 'Can I talk to you while you work?'

He shrugged. 'If you've got the stomach for it.'

She followed him into the centre, making mental notes of what she saw: a basic desk in front of a clapboard partition covered with notices; an animal weighing station, and three plastic chairs, two of them upended.

'That's it? No computers, monitors?' said Tina.

'Confiscated by your lot.'

'CCTV?'

'You're joking, right?'

A segregated area at the back housed ten animal cages; seven empty, three occupied. Two dogs looked up, eyelids heavy. The third yapped and barked, bouncing in his cage. She pinched her nose at the aroma of dog shit.

He looked at her with a semi-apologetic shrug. 'Been no chance to muck them out.'

She nodded. 'They've got to be put down? You can't take them to your hospital?'

'Nope. Beyond capacity.'

'And this place?'

He flicked his fingers across his neck in a slit-throat gesture.

'Shame.'

'Here,' he said, opening the door to the terrier bouncing in his cage. 'This one's a lunatic. Can you hold him by the scruff while I sedate him? That's it, good'. He shoved a needle into its flank.

While the vet turned his attention to the other two dogs, doing what must be done, she stroked the little terrier, his shaggy fur soft beneath her fingers. He held his bandaged front paw up in a shake-hands position, his expression quizzical, with one ear erect and the other folded forward in a flap.

Something nagged at Tina.

The dog wobbled, then lay down, getting comfortable. He rested his head on the floor of the cage, between his front paws, but continued to watch her, his brown eyes trusting.

This dog and Quin. A photo. Lavinia cooing. *Please, Mum*. Tina's heart beat a little faster.

She felt the vet's presence at her side. The other two cages were now empty.

'Just need to do this last one,' he said.

Fuck it. 'Can I take him?' she said.

'What?'

'Can I take him? Adopt him, whatever.'

He frowned at her. 'Like an impulse buy? I don't—'

'He's a bit short on other options.'

He read her face and saw what she was unable to articulate. 'Alright,' he said with a quick smile. 'He should have antibiotics. The police have confiscated everything.'

'I'll sort it. There's one more thing.' She told him that Quin believed that he and Ben had been attacked by the City Riflemen, after the dog cull, and she explained about the other dog, the dead one with the bullet hole that she'd bagged up riverside, 'It requires proper storage in a pathology mortuary, ASAP.' she said. 'And I might not get it past the officers by my car, whereas your van's right inside the zone. You could—'

'Take it in my van, to my hospital mortuary? Like I'm a fucking delivery service?'

'Kind of.'

'But, for what?'

'If we can retrieve a bullet—'

'We? You mean me?'

She gave him a long look.

He scratched his chin. 'Well... I guess if it might help Quin—'

'Thank you.'

'I wouldn't be tampering with evidence would I?'

'No way. I picked it up outside the taped area. Where's your phone?'

He jerked his thumb towards the desk.

She aimed her device and clicked 'New Contact.'

'I'll message you. Can I take him now?'

He lifted out the dog and, when he placed him in Tina's arms, she cradled his warm body like he was a sleeping baby. He snorted a little before settling into the deep sighs of sedation, and his breath was not unlike that of her teenage son on the days that he'd overslept for school and she'd awakened him.

'I'll call you Fiver,' she whispered.

ELLE BLAIR

Elle Blair teaches English to students who have been excluded from mainstream education. She loves police procedurals: hers focuses on the tension and humour which arise from juggling roles as a professional, a parent and a person. She lives by the sea in Whitley Bay with her family. *Adrift* is her first novel.

elleblairwriter@gmail.com

Adrift

An extract from a novel.

They told DI Rachel Harlow that this 5* cruise would take her mind off her impending disciplinary process. They were wrong.

CHAPTER SIX – SEA

Head pounding, Harlow slunk into the Riviera restaurant. The air outside as she'd raced across the ship had felt far too close. Storm clouds were gathering and darkness drawing in. She scanned the relaxed faces, all enjoying their sub-Michelin fare, across the white-clothed tables. Queasy with self-loathing, she took a deep breath before approaching her group.

'Mam!' At least Jess and Jake looked pleased to see her.

Her dad stood up. 'You had us worried, love.'

'Sorry,' she said. 'No reception. Lost track of the time.'

'For three hours?' Barbara's face was tight. Her lips were non-existent, clenched in an icy chokehold.

'Have a seat,' her dad said. 'We're just finishing, but go ahead and order.'

'No, no,' she said. 'I grabbed something downstairs.' Her stomach rumbled, as if to draw attention to the fact that she was a liar as well as a complete and utter disappointment.

Harlow sat in silence, watching her family eat the remains of their celebratory first night dinner. She was hot with shame. Knives and forks scraped across square plates. Conflicting smells emanating from people's meals in all directions made her want to heave.

The excruciating tension was eventually broken by Barbara. 'Come along, then. See if there are still any seats. We'll be right at the back, no doubt. Tyler and Danielle always draw a huge audience.'

'Tyler and Danielle?' Harlow said. 'That's who we're seeing?'

Her mum sighed. 'The headline act, Rachel.'

It was all coming back to her now. The YouTube audition. The judges' comments. The tan. The teeth. Up close, they had both aged on their meteoric rise to D-list celebrity status, but she understood now why he had seemed familiar.

'Are you not feeling well, love?' her dad asked. 'You've gone a funny colour.'

'Perfect,' she said, swallowing her nausea.

As they made their way across the room, she registered a cold voice in her ear,

'Your top is on inside out.' Harlow turned and met her mother's frosty gaze. Her look of disgust said more than a thousand words.

***

The house lights were dimming in the auditorium as the usher showed them to the few remaining seats. Walking behind Jess, Harlow noticed that she had defiantly stuck to her screw-the-patriarchy dress code; she looked great in her high-waisted jeans and crop top, but stood out a tad against the older, refined passengers. She was surprised that Barbara had entertained Jess's anti-regulation ensemble, but presumably, in the maelstrom of her own MIA status, they'd had bigger fish to fry.

Her lanky, gawky Jake had actually followed Gran's instructions and scrubbed himself up for the occasion. That made her want to cry. He was wearing his one and only pair of smart trousers and the deck shoes she'd forced upon him in Next before they'd left Newcastle. She wanted to reach out and squeeze his hand, but he'd already taken his seat.

Harlow had dived into the restrooms en route to recoup the last of her dignity and put her top on the right way round. It wasn't much, but it would have to do.

Her head pounded as the band crashed into action. The metallic thunk of the bass drum felt like it had been wired directly into her brain. She took a quick gulp of the white wine in her hand; she was going to need something to dilute the horror of watching the virtual stranger she had just had balls-deep in her mouth, now perform live for her multi-generational family.

A chorus line of identikit female dancers flounced around the stage, making patterns with oversize ostrich feathers, Vegas-style. Harlow was one row back from the rest of the family, hiding in the warm, dark anonymity. Barbara's pursed lips must have thawed out. She watched her mum crane her neck along the row of seats to say something to Jake.

A wave of tiredness washed over her. Maybe she could just rest her eyes for a moment. But, as the band reached a volume that could surely be heard back in Southampton, the dancers took their positions, feathers pointed inwards, shielding the middle of the stage. A booming voice emanated from the PA system, jolting Harlow back to life:

'Ladies and Gentlemen, for the fourth consecutive season on board the Harmony, we welcome our multi-award-winning Ballroom duo; the stage sensation, who Simon Cowell called, "my favourite EVER dance act"; the fabulous, the incomparable... Tyler Tweedy and Danielle Paige!'

Applause erupted like lava from Vesuvius. People were on their feet. Young girls screamed. A pair of women, really old enough to know better, were holding a 'We LOVE You Tyler!' banner. Jess turned around in her seat and gave her a sarcastic jazz-hands wave. Harlow did one back, trying to re-bond and make up for her earlier disappearing act.

The ostrich feathers parted to reveal the 'incomparable' Tyler and Danielle in a classic Latin hold, displaying the split in Danielle's neon outfit to its absolute max. Her legs, it had to be said, were extremely impressive. As were Tyler's rock-solid chest and abs, right there on display for all to see, with his lycra shirt cut down to the tightest pair of trousers she had ever seen.

The band launched into Tom Jones' 'Sex Bomb'. Harlow blinked: her reaction kept veering between belly-laughter at the cringetastic aesthetic and admiration for Tyler's incredible body moving in a blur of kicks, flicks and hip rotations. She looked around and took in the sea of captivated faces. She'd smirked, only a few hours ago, at his assessment of his status on board as 'kind of a big deal'. If anything, he had undersold himself. Tyler and Danielle were clearly very big fish indeed.

The cha-cha-cha opening number climaxed with an explosion of glitter. It rained down from the ceiling like the fallout from Hiroshima. Even from her position at the back of the auditorium, Harlow could feel herself ingesting sparkly particles of dance magic. She covered her wine in alarm and took another big gulp.

Tyler and Danielle swished off stage to rapturous applause whilst the ostrich girls returned, featherless, for some more filler. After an astonishingly tight turnaround, the stars were back, dressed in completely different costumes, accompanied by the opening notes of a pared-down, moody version of Sting's 'Roxanne'. Danielle was in an eye-wateringly tight, red floor-length gown this time, again with her signature thigh-high split. Tyler was all in black, a waistcoat skimming his rippling muscles.

Harlow felt herself flushing at the thought of what she could still have been doing with him downstairs, below the water line.

The room was pitch black, save for a spotlight, which followed the duo as they tangled and untangled their limbs seamlessly in a series of sharp, staccato beats. This was actually good, she conceded, the two bodies a passionate blur of skin on skin. On the edge of her seat now, she held her glass unsteadily between her knees as the routine ended with a dramatic drop, Danielle caught by Tyler in a tight grip with their faces intensely aligned, almost in a kiss.

Instinctively, she joined the roar of the crowd. The lights lifted, illuminating Tyler and Danielle, arms raised. They smiled at each other adoringly. There was not a trace of the anger and threat which had characterised their interaction downstairs. Harlow downed the remains of her glass, trying to stave off the sensation of the room spinning. If she just kept drinking, she would at least have a distraction. She wondered if she could sneak out and get a refill.

Each holding a microphone, Tyler and Danielle faced the audience.

'Thank you so much for your incredible reception!' Danielle said, hand theatrically on her heart. Her voice was nothing like the shrieking banshee of an hour ago.

'We're so excited to be here with you tonight on the *Harmony of the Seas*!' Tyler boomed. His energy seemed more appropriate for a sell-out Wembley show than a floating theatre somewhere between Southampton and Spain. Maybe, like Danielle, he was partial to a chemical boost before a show. From her experience of policing taxi queues, she would have put money on the cause of his gurning expression.

'If you're enjoying the show, we wanted to remind you that we have our extremely popular *Dance with Tyler and Danielle* workshops running throughout the voyage. But spaces are limited, aren't they, Tyler?'

'They certainly are, Danielle. And we wouldn't want anyone to miss out, so get it booked!'

'Should we give them a sneak preview?'

'Let's do it!' They beamed at the crowd.

'Tyler and I pride ourselves that we can teach *anyone* to dance. You might think you've got two left feet, but don't let that put you off!'

'That's right, Danielle. And you can book as a couple or just come along solo – remember strangers on the *Harmony* are simply friends you haven't met yet. Isn't that right, guys?'

The audience whooped enthusiastically. These two really had them eating out of the palm of their hands, Harlow marvelled. It was like a cult.

'Shall we get a couple of beautiful people from our wonderful audience up here and show everyone what we can do in only ten minutes?'

Mics in hand, the dance sensations strode down the steps and made their way into the auditorium. Harlow shuffled further down in her chair.

'So many eager volunteers!' Danielle trilled. 'However, what we really need is two slightly more reluctant performers. If you don't know your quickstep from your rumba, this is the moment to learn –'

'That's right Danielle, it's a once-in-a-lifetime moment to shine!' Tyler was walking dangerously close to her part of the room now. She craned her head away and tried to make herself morph into the red velvet chair.

'I've spotted a perfect dancer-to-be!' called Tyler. 'She's trying to avoid eye contact, but here she is. Ladies and gentlemen, put your hands together for our first volunteer!'

Harlow closed her eyes tightly, bracing herself for catastrophe. And there it was: Tyler's hand stretching forwards from the aisle, gripping her arm and pulling her onto unsteady feet. She tried desperately to stay seated, but, as the audience erupted into ear-splitting applause, the strangers around her demonstrated almost-criminal levels of coercion and physical strength that belied their ageing limbs and previous decorum.

She was shunted forwards, legs feeling like they belonged to someone else, until she stood, horrified, next to Tyler. Jesus fucking Christ. Instinctively, she scrambled for her handcuffs, determined to regain control. But the relief of cold metal rings at her fingertips was gone. She was defenceless.

Tyler whispered into her ear, 'I couldn't resist, Sherlock.'

Booming again now, into his microphone, he addressed the audience. 'Our first dancer! Shall we find out her name, guys?'

As the crowd sounded their approval, Harlow looked desperately to her children, hoping they might stage an intervention. Jake shrugged, looking highly embarrassed, whilst Jess – the traitor - was creased over, hysterical with laughter, tears rolling down her cheeks. Her parents looked bemused, but again, offered no help whatsoever.

'It's Rachel,' she said, through gritted teeth. Her voice sounded hollow and far away. Maybe she was having an out-of-body experience. Up close, Tyler looked manic. His pupils were pinpricks: tiny dots jumping in front of her as his eyes darted around the crowd.

'Right, Danielle, let's get Rachel ready to dance!'

Defeated, she allowed herself to be led to the stage. The house lights dimmed and she was thrust into the spotlight next to an obese man in his fifties, *'the gorgeous Kevin',* whose shirt buttons strained as sweat dripped from his bald head.

Danielle looked her up and down, slowly, and flashed the fakest of fake smiles.

'So, can we teach them to dance, guys?' Tyler called into the crowd.

'YES!' came the deafening reply, accompanied by whistles and cheers.

Gripping with knife-sharp talons, Danielle embraced her rigid shoulders. She breathed into her ear, 'Stay away from Tyler, you slutty polis bitch,' before squeezing her warmly for the benefit of the audience and speaking into her microphone, 'A lady this beautiful needs a dress to dance in, do we agree?'

Danielle snatched a white, diamond-encrusted gown from the wings and skipped back into the spotlight where she held it aloft. 'Stunning!'

Harlow swayed as the nylon encased her body. The full skirt skimmed over her tight jeans, transforming her into a replica of the ostrich girls she had foolishly smirked at earlier. Dear God, when would this nightmare end? She felt exposed and worryingly nauseous.

Up close, she could see the deep scratch on Tyler's cheek, despite his heavy make-up. As Danielle arranged the skirt to its crystal light-catching perfection she saw a look of fury pass between them. Tiny, contained, but full of rage.

Tyler grinned, escorting her to the left of the stage, whilst Danielle and her victim moved to the right. His hand felt clammy, or was that coming from her own skin? The band kicked into a high-energy blast of something that sounded like Abba.

'With a bit of support, even the unlikeliest of dancers can become an elegant partner!' Danielle said, her empathetic voice juxtaposing with the death-stares she kept flashing in Harlow's direction.

'Just follow my lead, babe,' Tyler said to her, unmicced and intense.

She said nothing, mouth filling with saliva, as she concentrated on not tripping over the hem of the dress. Tyler spun her around, so her back was pressed into his body. His hand snaked up the inside of the dress. She blinked blindly into the glare, the audience invisible and felt something slide into her back pocket, a hard edge against her bum.

Tyler's voice again, low and muffled, 'Let yourself in later, babe. I want out. I'm gonna give you all of it, ok?'

Harlow swallowed, desperately trying to stop the rising nausea, but it fought back against her clenched throat, uncontrollable now, as the music surged to its crescendo. A powerful motion rocked her body and she felt vomit explode into the air, landing with a splat, centre stage, spraying Danielle and The Gorgeous Kevin with six hours' worth of all-inclusive drinking.

It could have been her imagination, but she was sure she heard her mother's scream as the music stopped abruptly and she fled the decimated stage.

CHAPTER SEVEN

Harlow couldn't see straight as she ran through the wings, tripping on the trailing hem. Lungs constricted with humiliation, she could hardly breathe as she willed herself forward. Now in the backstage corridor, she used every last ounce of sobriety to find a way out of this labyrinth of shame.

She ached for a silent corner where she could just lie down and black out for the foreseeable future. But the small, police officer's voice in the very back of her mind knew she needed to get outside, to fresh air, to a place where she could expunge the rest of the liquid swashing around her stomach.

After what felt like a marathon of patterned carpets and strangers' stares, she burst through the double doors onto the top deck. Wind and rain smacked her in the face. She stood there, still for a moment, just letting the water fall. Grabbing the nearest polished railing, she felt the sweet relief of oblivion as the remaining alcohol left her body, thundering into the waves below.

The last time she'd been sick from drinking was the CID Christmas party, where she'd had to be forcibly removed from a karaoke bar by Lennon, to save the general public from a third Whitney Houston number, murdered in her own unique style. He'd put her to bed in her clothes and slept on the sofa just to check she wasn't about to choke on her own bile.

She missed him. His warmth, a million miles away.

Clumsily, with fingers which wouldn't follow simple commands, she located WhatsApp and pressed Call. An unfamiliar ringtone sounded. She waited, stomach clenching, not knowing what she wanted to say. A crackle and then his unmistakable, laid-back tone, 'Alright?'

'Lenn – are you there?' She snorted back the sobs which were threatening to come rushing out.

'You ok? All – crackly – hear – too well.'

'Did I wake you up? What time is it?'

'S'alright. Yeah – bed – worry about -, though.'

'You sure? Sorry I've woken you. I'm sorry for everything.'

'- talkin' about? Sorry – what?'

'The arrest. Professional Standards.' She winced. 'I've dragged you down with me.'

' - - man, - - bother. You sound - -, sure you're –'

'The worst night. Made a total fool of myself. I've let everyone down, Lenn.' Her voice sounded thick and slurred; she couldn't get her lips to catch up with her tongue.

'You're breaking up – didn't catch – say again–'

'I've been awful.'

His voice clicked back into clarity. 'You're always awful, man. That's why we love you so much.'

'Do you, though?'

'Can't – anything. - - standing in - hurricane?'

She breathed in, trying to control the pain in her chest. In for three, out for three. The way they did with people who'd been stabbed.

'—chel? –chel? You ok? You – the kids?'

'I'll be ok. Go back to sleep. I'll find some better reception tomorrow.' Her voice caught in her throat.

'—off the deck, – inside. It – be late where you are. – yourself to bed.'

'Ok. Bye.' The line went dead.

She looked down at her phone, water bouncing off its cracked screen. The white dress was sodden now, dragging heavily as she turned around to follow his advice.

She almost walked straight into her mum, who came clattering through the entrance, red in the face and wild-eyed. Harlow died a little inside. She had been hoping to make her apologies and start picking up the pieces after a few hours' sleep. By then, Barbara's disapproval might have receded somewhat on the Richter scale.

'Rachel – why? What makes you behave like this?'

Right, they were going straight into it. No preamble.

'I don't know what you want me to say. I know I've fucked up, ok?'

'Your language, Rachel! The children just mimic you. Your dad's had to take them back to your cabin. And I've been all over, high and low, looking for you.'

'Have we not got bigger issues? I mean, for fuck's sake, Mum. Pick your battles.'

'I don't know where we went wrong. We tried our best.' Barbara's voice cracked. She pulled a handkerchief from her sleeve and dabbed her eyes.

'You were fine. You *are* fine. I'm just going through a rough patch. Things are getting on top of me. I wanted to forget about it all, just for one night.'

'But you've got responsibilities! Two children. Bills to pay.'

'I know! *I'm* not a child. And we get by.'

'You were straight back there. As soon as you knew, you were just waiting to leave us.'

'Why d'you always bring that up?' She could feel herself losing it. 'I wanted to find out where I'd come from. Who I was. Why can't you accept that?'

'I *tried*, Rachel. I tried to make you mine.' Barbara's voice rose to a wail. Her carefully made-up face and respectable demeanour was falling apart in front of her eyes.

'You shouldn't have to *try* though, should you,' she bit back. 'Loving your daughter shouldn't be a fucking effort.'

'And neither should loving your mother!'

She fought to hold back her rage. But it was coming. It had been coming for so long and there was nothing she could do now to stop it. 'You're not my mother, though, are you? You're not anyone's mother.'

She watched Barbara stumble as if she'd been slapped and clutch the railing for support. Her eyes were wide; stripped-back, raw flesh was exposed beneath her tightly pinched skin.

Harlow stepped forwards, holding out an unsteady hand, 'I shouldn't have said that –'

Barbara gathered herself, trying to push the rain away from her linen trouser suit. It was drenched to a completely different shade from its original biscuit tone, creased and crumpled, worn out and shapeless.

Harlow's hand shook in her fragile attempt at reconciliation. Barbara said nothing, her own arms rigid by her sides. The fire of their conversation had subsided, damp embers lying between them on the rain-soaked floor. The space between them was cold again. With a final wounded look, Barbara walked away, handkerchief trailing like a white flag with no use anymore.

Harlow allowed her misery to engulf her. She drifted hopelessly up the deck, heading nowhere. Nothing was going to repair the damage she'd inflicted tonight. She was completely alone. The lashing rain knifed her like a thousand tiny incisions. She kept her feet moving mechanically, one in front of the other, until she found herself leaning over a railing, hardly able to tell what was sea and what was sky. It was all oily blackness. A void in every direction.

Hoisting herself higher, body slumped over the barrier, she felt unexpected relief at being closer to the crashing waves. The sights and sounds of the abyss were in perfect symmetry to the swirling emotion inside. She imagined letting herself fall, the quick and absolute embrace of the water.

She lifted one finger, and then another, exhausted beyond measure, slowly releasing herself from the storm.

CHAPTER EIGHT

She loosened her grip, felt herself sliding. But a sound made her stop. A crackle of feedback. A firm American voice.

'Would all passengers please return to their cabins. We are currently experiencing a period of inclement weather, and, for health and safety reasons, we ask all passengers to return to their cabins immediately.'

Harlow let go of the railing and fell backwards onto the hard floor, gripping her banging head with both hands. She could almost see Jess and Jake, shadowy and much younger, sinking into the blackness, somewhere far away in her mind. She willed herself to reach out to them.

It felt real: Jess holding her hand tightly, Jake's outstretched fingertips just brushing her own. Clinging to the image, she forced her body upwards.

Finding her way back, with regret oozing from every pore, was a Herculean effort, but the windowless cabin was a relief, once she was inside, protected from the elements. Jess and Jake were still awake, but muted. They'd turned on the virtual balcony, so they all sat, huddled tightly, watching grey sky battle grey water. They didn't ask where she'd been. Jake wordlessly handed her a cup of tea with two sugars. Jess's phone beeped: Grandad checking that their mum had returned.

Harlow's own phone was silent.

She swallowed down a lump in her throat: those moments on the deck, her near descent into the crashing water. She had let them down. But, she was here. And maybe it wasn't too late to start again. As her eyelids began to droop, she reached over and tucked them both in a bit tighter, duvets snug around their shoulders. She turned out the lamp and let herself be carried away, bobbing softly into the silence of sleep.

***

The tannoy woke Harlow: its velvet tone making her open one eye groggily, wondering where she was.

'Due to the ongoing adverse weather conditions as we cross the Bay of Biscay, we request that passengers remain inside and do not use the outdoor decks. A further announcement will be made in due course, when we will be delighted to re-open the full facilities.'

The room was unfamiliar, with a strange rumble coming from behind her back. It sounded like Jess. She shivered, and yanked another sliver of duvet. Picking up her phone from the floor, she checked the time: 09:15. The windowless box was dark and still; if she hadn't had a clock, it would be impossible to tell if it were night or day.

More clues were needed. Gingerly, testing her hangover, she tip-toed around the room, picking up discarded clothes. The white gown was still damp; her jeans were also not looking their best. She fished out a key card from the pocket and was rapidly transported back to Tyler's words in her ear, urging her to let herself into Cabin 656, his hands everywhere under the dress.

'Y'alright, Mam,' came a croaky voice. 'How you feeling?' It was Jake, rubbing his eyes and yawning.

'Not too bad,' she said. 'You?'

'Yeah. Alright. What time is it?'

'It's about nine. We've got to stay inside though til the storm blows over.'

He sat up. 'Is that normal?'

'No idea. I'm sure the captain's got it covered. I'm not dying to get back out there, though.'

'You weren't that bad.'

'I was. I'm really sorry you saw me in that state.'

'What d'you mean? I'm buzzing. You can literally never have a go at me in the future for getting mortal.'

'True.' She smiled, and he gave her a lopsided grin.

Another rumble from Jess shook the room. Jake picked up his phone and videoed the inhuman noises.

'What you gonna do with that? She'll kill you, mind.'

'Just good to have a bit of insurance in the bank.' He nodded sagely, then dived onto the bed and squished his face into his twin sister's. She let out a scream as she opened her eyes.

'Mam – get him off me! His breath stinks.'

'This footage is absolute gold,' said Jake. 'Your snoring's going viral.'

Jess sat bolt upright and tried to grab the phone off him. 'You wouldn't dare.'

'Try me.' He grinned, twisting out of her grip.

***

The morning of captivity within the cabin crawled. Hours of channel hopping, playing cards and listening to Jake's increasingly plaintive requests for food. At the point where cannibalism was seeming like a viable possibility, another tannoy sounded and they were given the all-clear.

Jake was only interested in eating, while Jess wanted to find a hot tub. They compromised on filling their faces in the all-day buffet, before locating an array of jacuzzies looking out to sea.

After skulking around for five minutes on the periphery and eyeballing everyone, a couple got the hint and vacated one of the pools. Harlow leant back against the powerful jets and tried to stop her mind from diverting back to last night. From here they could watch the now-calm sea stretching to the shimmering horizon, but she didn't feel relaxed; she felt restless.

She'd dropped Tyler's key card into her bag when they'd left the cabin, and as she sat, simmering in the bubbly water, she wondered whether she should just rip the plaster off.

Assuring Jess and Jake she'd be back in half an hour max, she threw a sarong over her bikini and took a deep breath. Yes, she'd thrown up live on stage right next to someone she'd just gone down on, but wasn't that all water under the bridge now?

And besides, nine inches was nine inches. It was always good to leave your options open.

She located the staff lift, using the key card to retrace her steps. Pausing for a second outside his cabin, she knocked and waited. There was no answer, so she knocked again, louder. She considered the legality of just popping her head in. Given the key card, there would be no use of force required, negating the potential of a breaking and entering accusation. That left only trespassing. And, as she'd had a very enthusiastic invitation only a few hours ago to let herself in, she decided to take that as permission granted. A tiny click was all it took against the card reader to gently push the door open.

'Tyler?' she called quietly, crossing the threshold. 'I just wanted to apologise for last nigh-' The word expired on her lips. His body was slumped forwards. The acrid smell of shit in the air, along with the unnatural position of his head told Harlow more than half the contents of any coroner's report. She dropped to her knees, pressing two fingers to his wrist.

Nothing.

His eyes were open, but unblinking; dilated, blank pupils stared into the distance, refusing to give her any insight into what on earth had happened in here last night. Come on - *think*, she told herself. CID training. Assume nothing; believe no-one; challenge everything. Position of the body suggested a sudden loss of consciousness. Grey pallor and stench in the air pointed to a time of death nearer yesterday than today.

In the absence of gloves, she wrapped the edge of the sarong around her hand and carefully raised Tyler's head a few inches from the floor. His lips had a horrible bluish tinge. The dried foam at his mouth and the powder remnants in the plastic wrap beneath his body were unsurprising. The colour, though, was odd. A brownish shadow. He'd been the headliner; surely he wouldn't have been snorting any old shite.

There was something stuck to the outside of the plastic, too. A tiny opaque disc, folded over on itself, barely the size of her smallest fingernail. She followed a trickle of blood from the corner of his mouth, peeling back his cold lips to find a savage laceration at the front of his tongue. A fit, then? Some sort of seizure?

Decisively, she pulled out her phone and took pictures of the key exhibits, Tyler's body and a wider shot of the room: bare, anonymous and devoid of personality. Avoiding touching anything more, she ran for the corridor, hammering on doors and shouting into the ether for some sort of back-up.

No-one came.

Tyler was dead. And now she was going to have to explain why the fuck she was down here, first on the scene, with a body on her hands.

G.M. CHIVES

G. M. Chives, a linguist and a medievalist, is originally from Italy. She gained a PhD at Cardiff University. She is a lecturer and has worked for the Italian Ministry of Foreign Affairs in Asia and Europe. She's published short stories in Italy, and academic works in English and Italian. She now lives between England and Italy.

antelmi.g@gmail.com

The Bee Van

The opening of a novel

CHAPTER ONE – THE CRUELLEST MONTH
April 2010, Reykjavík, Iceland

'I've got to get off this island as soon as possible!' The woman, phone clutched in hand and waterproof jacket folded over arm, leant forward over the travel agent's counter.

'You're on the waiting list, Ms Berio. As you know, all flights have been suspended. If a seat becomes available, you'll be contacted.' The travel agent grabbed a selection of leaflets from the stand near the computer. 'I'm sure there are tourist attractions that you haven't yet visited during your stay here in Reykjavík.' A hint of a smile formed on her face. 'Here at the top, you'll also find information about the Icelandic Phallological Museum. It's unique. Not every tourist brochure lists it.' She pushed the leaflets forward.

Carlotta Berio looked at the travel agent. The badge pinned to her lapel read Hilda. She was neatly attired in a navy-blue uniform, her ink black hair gathered tightly at the nape of her neck. Behind her was a poster depicting a ferry sailing away from the coast towards the open sea. In the backdrop, a gentle chain of green mountains.

Carlotta took a deep breath. 'Look, Ms Hilda. It seems to me we haven't understood each other. It's a *real* emergency. I've got to get back.'

'The volcano is throwing out clouds of debris, making flights impossible. The situation is unfolding as we speak.' Hilda held the tourist material in mid-air.

'I know all that.' Carlotta sighed. 'I know all these people want to go home.' She pointed to the mass of people funnelled between the queue barriers who filled the office. 'For me it's a question of life or –' Carlotta paused, weighing the words she was about to utter.

Her father's voice from their last phone call two days earlier revolved in her mind. 'The doctors say your mother hasn't much time left.' The moment this conversation was over, her race against time began, against the dust cloud, against the competition and demands of other travellers who were all impatient to leave Iceland.

'My mother's in hospital critically ill. Her life is hanging by a thread,' said Carlotta. 'What waiting list have you put me down on?'

'Air France, the airline you flew in with. Standard class.'

'I want you to put me on *all* the lists. *Every* airline flying to Europe, to the UK, it doesn't matter. Standard, First, Business class, whatever. I just need to leave.' Carlotta saw that the employee raised her eyebrows at this. 'Do you want to see that I can pay?' She thumped her rucksack on to the counter.

Hilda put down the leaflets.

'What I'm asking you now is to look at your screen and find me the first available seat, with any airline. Any destination. Any fare!' Carlotta put her Platinum credit card in front of her.

Hilda tapped the keyboard, eyes fixed forward.

Carlotta turned to the images displayed on a large television screen on the wall. The volcano was spewing out a thick black cloud into the sky. She had come to Reykjavik to see the venue for her next exhibition, to meet Ms Asa Guðrún Magnúsdóttir, the art gallery curator, and discuss the event. A couple of weeks ago she had been thrilled that Geneviève, the gallery director in Paris, had invited her along. At the time she had no idea that her mother was unwell. Had her father kept it from her? Had it happened all of a sudden?

'Even if the flights resume, everything is fully booked for the next two weeks at least,' said Hilda. 'I'm afraid we can't give you priority over the passengers who are already booked on these flights.'

'What about ferries to mainland Europe?' Carlotta pointed to the poster on the wall.

'There is a weekly ferry service that has just resumed after winter, leaving from Seyðisfjörður for Denmark. It takes three days.'

'Three days!'

Hilda looked up from her monitor. 'For the whole of this month every place is taken.'

'What about private boats?' Carlotta tapped the counter with her card.

'I can't help you there. I'm sorry.' Hilda's sentence came out pat as if she were a speaking doll.

No, Hilda, Carlotta thought. You aren't sorry. Your face expresses neither sympathy nor sorrow. Carlotta knew too well the signs of sorrow and suffering. She had often observed them. They showed themselves on the faces of the people who used to sit in front of her on the *Promenade des Anglais* in Nice to have their portrait done. That seemed like a lifetime away. Another existence. Twenty years ago, she used to commute from her hometown, Bracausi, the Italian town on the border, in her old Fiat 500 with her charcoal and paper, a couple of chairs and a folding table. Tourists strolling along the *Promenade* would willingly take time out, sit down in the warmth of the sun, and have their portrait drawn.

Hilda gave her a textbook 'Is there anything else I can do for you?' She picked up the same tourist material as before and held it out.

Carlotta shook her head and left it in Hilda's hand.

She drifted towards the front window. She caught a glimpse of her reflection and passed a hand through her dishevelled hair, then looked out. The blue sky, thinly veiled with lavender, gave no indication that just a hundred kilometres away the Roman God Vulcan was in a state of fury. Or rather a Nordic divinity, now raging. Loki, perhaps. Whatever was brewing underground, she was now stranded. Barriers can be of many kinds, even dust, she thought. She tapped on her phone. Her mother's face was smiling as she cut her birthday cake, the number seventy-eight decorated on top. Carlotta swiped on. The next picture was a close-up of the two of them, heads together as they hugged and smiled. She swiped again, and again. The photos were taken mostly in the kitchen. Her mother had no space that was hers. Her only private place was her mind.

There were thoughts that her mother wouldn't share. There were times Carlotta had found her tidying up, eyes swollen. 'What's the matter?' 'Nothing,' she would answer, wiping her eye. Her mother would avoid one particular conversation, wriggling out of it saying: 'We'll talk about it another time.' Her father wanted to arrange their fiftieth wedding anniversary celebration with their friends and include the priest. Her mother categorically refused. A few days before the date, she said she didn't feel well. She wasn't strong enough to leave the flat. When Carlotta went into her bedroom, she found her immersed in *The House of Spirits*, the novel her mother loved to return to. Deep down, Carlotta felt that there was something unsaid that had to pass down from her mother to her.

Last week, had Carlotta known about her mother's deteriorating health, she would never have left Paris and come here with Geneviève. It wasn't necessary that she was here at all. She was now regretting having jumped at Geneviève's idea. In the past few days, she had visited art galleries with inspiring collections, appreciated the flavour of *Smørbrød*, enjoyed the long daylight hours and admired the dramatic lunar landscape. However, Geneviève, whom she trusted blindly, could have organised the forthcoming event without her. Even more so given that all Carlotta's projects were under an assumed name. In her art milieu no one knew her other identity. As Carlotta Berio, she was just a teacher employed at a small private school in Paris. It pained her that she kept it secret even from her mother. As time was running out, she felt willing to tell her. Maybe her mother would be willing to open up too.

Now the eruption of the Eyjafjallajökull volcano had curtailed travel throughout Europe, Carlotta wanted to sink into darkness. Just sink. She thought of the whiskey bar from the night before. She would go back there, submerge herself in its dimness and let her stomach, her chest vibrate, her heart throb to the rhythm of the heavy bass, and stun herself with whiskey and shots of Icelandic vodka, *brennivín*. Any form of alcohol which would prevent her thoughts from torturing her mind would do.

She scrolled down her phone to find Geneviève's number. She would be at Keflavik airport trying to find a seat.

On the second ring, Geneviève answered, 'Otta, *chérie, désolée.*' Only Carlotta's close friends called her Otta. 'It's total confusion. Flights are still grounded. And before you ask, no private planes.'

'Nothing here either.' Carlotta sighed.

'Any news from Italy?'

'No news.'

'Otta, let's meet back at the hotel, *alors*. A sauna might do us some good and divert our thoughts. *Bisous, chérie*.' Geneviève hung up.

Carlotta turned away from the window. She felt powerless. There was nothing she could do. She was stuck on the island. Carlotta had spent the last forty-eight hours, ever since her father's first call, with her phone glued to her hand, first at the airport, here at the travel agent, and in bed in the wonderful suite on the top floor. The eye mask provided by her five-star hotel couldn't protect her from her worst nightmare: not being able to see her mother one more time. She sat down on a chair and leant forward, elbows on thighs. In these two days, the phone had become something to hold on to. Carlotta had started to hear it ring even when there were no real calls, just phantom ones. She kept on checking. The television on the wall was now spitting out images of events that were being cancelled across Europe, concerts, sport and political meetings, some planned months in advance, years even. A carousel of images: the volcano, close-ups of Barack Obama, of Angela Merkel shifted on the screen. Both were unable to attend President Lech Kaczyński's funeral in Poland.

The phone vibrated. Carlotta sprang up, moved away from the noise of the customers, finding a quiet corner. She stuck her shoulders back, bracing herself against the wall. Her fingertip slid the green symbol across. She listened, breath held.

'Carlotta, can you hear me?'

'Yes, I can. Hi, Dad.'

A short silence followed. Carlotta heard her father breathing.

'Your mother is no longer here with us. She passed away this morning.'

Otta retreated further into the corner. Her gaze fixed on the row of empty chairs in front of her.

'Did you hear me?' Her father's voice sounded imperious.

'Yes, yes. I did.' She brought a hand up to cover her lips.

He sounded matter of fact. How could he, Carlotta wondered, utter those words without his voice betraying even a hint of emotion?

'The funeral is on Friday, in four days.'

'Four days?' She gasped. 'That's not possible.' She gathered all her strength to speak. 'I can't make it there in time. We need to postpone. I'm stuck here. There's no planes, no transport. Nothing. Didn't you hear the news?'

'Why the hell did you go there, to that god-forsaken place?'

'I told you. I'm here for work,' she said, although she had never really told him anything about her work, her life.

'I've left it in the hands of the funeral director, Iacometti. He's already fixed the date. I'm just letting you know.'

'It can't be so soon. I need time to get there. Are you listening to me?'

'You left here for good. Too bad.'

'I'll speak with Iacometti myself.'

'There's nothing to discuss. And I don't have money to waste on international calls. To Iceland or wherever you choose to be.'

'I'll call you back. We need to talk about it.'

'It's all been decided.'

The phone screen went black. He had hung up.

Calling Iacometti would be pointless. She knew it. He was a friend of her father's and wouldn't go against his plans.

Carlotta couldn't comprehend. How could this happen? Until a few seconds ago, her worst nightmare was not being able to see her mother, speak to her again. She slid down the wall, her legs no longer supporting her. Her knees bent under her weight. She crouched low in the corner, in disbelief. And now that nightmare had become nothing compared to what was unfolding before her now. Missing her mother's funeral?

CHAPTER 2 – NEIGHBOURS BY CHANCE
January 2012, Bracausi, Italy

A sudden gust of cold wind hit Carlotta. She wrapped herself up in her ice-white coat and tightened the belt. She was standing in front of the wall where names were carved into marble. High above, the tops of cypresses swayed across segments of blue sky. The birds sang unperturbed in conversation from the branches: for them, here or in any other tree, there was no difference. After the dawn storm, the smell of earth lingered, now puddles reflected the brightness of the sun like mirrors. Her eyes returned to the imposing wall of square marble plaques, each covering a burial recess. To her, it was like a block of flats. Here too people cohabited by chance. On each plaque the name, the date of entry and departure from this world. Just like a play on the stage, characters entered and exited. In life, one is at times an actor, at times a spectator. Even a protagonist can't decide every turn in the plot. On her right, not far from her, an elderly man talked quietly to the photograph affixed to the marble. Farther away at the end of the wall, a woman equipped with marigold gloves busied herself arranging fresh flowers in a metal vase.

Carlotta turned to face the two inscriptions in front of her. She followed the letters and numbers as a child would, learning to read.

Cesare Berio, July 1930-December 2011

Marta Berio née Conti, September 1930-April 2010

Her mother, her serene expression and kind smile, looked out from the oval photograph as out of a window from another world into this. Cesare held his stern look, his thin lips slightly stretched but not enough to form a smile. Don't weaken your masculinity by smiling.

'See you tomorrow,' said the elderly man waving towards the photo. He turned to Carlotta, 'I've made my daily visit to my wife. I always tell her what I've been up to. You know, after a life spent together, I can't suddenly stop talking to her. I'm certain she's watching over me.'

What's the point in telling her what you've been doing, then, Carlotta thought. 'When did you lose her?' she asked, instead.

'Just gone eleven months. You don't come here very often, do you? The flowers are plastic.' He jutted his chin towards the wall.

You like playing Sherlock Holmes, she thought. 'Just like neighbours, we have different routines,' she said.

'See you soon,' said the man. To which woman the greeting was addressed was not clear.

She turned back to her parents, intent on standing there a few more moments to avoid walking back alongside the man. The noise of trodden gravel made her look round. On seeing who it was, she returned her focus to the marble. The dark blue silhouette of a police uniform sidled up to her.

'They're not here, Enrico,' she said.

'Who's not here, Otta?'

'It feels good. A friendly voice calling me that.' After a brief silence she added, '*They*, my parents aren't here.' She pointed to her mother's photo. 'I'll never forgive myself.'

'You were stuck in Iceland, Otta. It wasn't your fault. You did what you possibly could.'

'Now it's only me. You spend your whole life looking for your real self, trying to shed your former skin and become who you are.' Otta sighed. She thought Enrico would understand her.

'Is this why you left for Paris?'

She was aware that she had to be careful about what she could say now that she was back in Bracausi, her hometown. 'How long have you been watching me, Enrico?'

'Let's go to my father,' he said.

They walked under the colonnades that sheltered people from the elements, turned left, climbed a flight of stairs and reached an open space where tombstones were regimented row upon row. They stopped in front of one where the face of a man in uniform with a gentle expression was centred above copper letters.

Pietro Rossi, November 1935-December 1984

'Inspector Enrico Rossi, your father would be proud of you.' Otta took Enrico by the arm. 'We were so young when he was killed. At the time I didn't understand the impact this has had on you. I'm so sorry.'

'No need to apologise. We're about his age now. It sounds unreal.'

Otta knew that Enrico was still burdened by his father's death.

'I always liked your father. He was warm and approachable, unusual for someone who was a police officer.' Otta squinted at Enrico. Hazelnut eyes, dark brown hair kept in check with a good dose of gel, strong jawline. 'You look so like him, but there's something of your mother too.'

'I've known you since we were children. I can tell that something is troubling you, Otta.'

'I know *you* too, and I recognize those two lines on your forehead. It's the policeman speaking now.' Otta left Enrico's arm. 'Is that why I keep on bumping into you? On the landing, in town?'

'We're neighbours. We're bound to meet. And you've forgotten what a small town Bracausi is. It's inevitable.'

'But here, at the cemetery? Are you following me?'

'There's been an incident nearby. A migrant drowned, Yousouf. We found his body on the beach, washed up after the storm.'

'You knew him.'

Enrico nodded. 'It wasn't an accident, I'm sure. He was troubled, he wanted to tell me something. And now he's dead. He's left a sister. I need to find her. I don't know why I'm telling you this.'

'And now you're here…?'

'Your car is parked outside. You're the only person driving a Figaro in the whole province. Anyway, what's bothering you?'

Otta was annoyed. 'Do you think your uniform gives you the right to pry?'

'It's not prying, Otta. Anita and I are your friends. We want to help.'

'I really appreciate your support. I don't know what I'd do without you two. But right now, I don't know who's speaking, a friend or a police officer.'

'A friend.'

She sighed. 'I believe you. What's there to tell you? You know I'm teaching art in Paris. A boring, ordinary life with little to tell.' Otta put her hand on Enrico's arm. 'Just give me some space. I need time on my own, that's all. I think I'll go for a walk on the beach now, to clear my head.'

Otta turned away. The heels of her boots resounded on the steps leading down to the exit. She didn't turn back though she could feel Enrico watching her. She ran through their conversation in her mind. No, she hadn't let anything slip and hopefully her expression had not betrayed her. She would defend her life she had created at all costs. She strode through the cemetery's iron gates towards her car. No one was going to intrude on her secret life in Paris.

CHAPTER 3 – DEATH BY WATER

The photograph of President Napolitano stared out from the frame on the wall, above the shoulder of *Commissario* Giordano. The legal tomes of the Law Codes filled the shelves of the bookcase, an Italian and a European flag in a corner. On his desk, a telephone with finger-worn keys, folders, a desktop calendar, scattered pens, and a framed picture.

'Inspector Rossi and Inspector Panzani, take a seat,' Giordano said.

'The sunset in this photograph is beautiful, Mr Giordano.'

'It's dawn, Panzani. Dawn. What did you learn at the Police school if you can't even distinguish east from west?' Giordano didn't lift his gaze from the folder he was thumbing through.

The dawn of one of those mornings so limpid that one could clearly see the outline of Corsica on the horizon. Enrico knew it was there that Giordano intended to retire, where people were happy to speak Italian. He wouldn't have to brush up on his French. An island, for him to leave everything behind, not look back. Giordano had talked about his dream countless times. Enrico knew it all by heart.

Giordano weighed his words, the skin hanging loose below his jaw moved slowly while he was ruminating. The thin lips parted to speak, as if he were about to mouth an oracle.

'Mohammed Yousouf Al Arawi.' Giordano's moist bovine eyes lifted up from the documents and fixed upon Enrico and his colleague Panzani. 'The autopsy establishes the cause of death as drowning, presumed suicide or misadventure.'

'Something doesn't add up,' said Enrico.

'Rossi, there are witnesses who state that this guy was extremely tense, agitated, that he couldn't stand being stuck in Italy any longer. There are two possibilities: either he lost all hope of getting into France and took his own life, or he was making a desperate attempt to swim across the border.'

Enrico knew from experience that when Giordano used his surname he was in no mood for objections.

'He was found wearing his swimming trunks,' said Panzani.

'That detail doesn't make sense,' Enrico said.

'Rossi, it was either foolishness or depression,' said Giordano.

'What do you mean, Rossi?' Panzani dragged his chair closer to the desk.

'Yousouf couldn't swim. He told me himself he was petrified on the boat in the Mediterranean. And anyway, he really cared for his sister. He just wouldn't have abandoned her.'

'Rossi, this was the state of mind of...' – Giordano searched in the folder – 'of this Mohammed months ago. Witnesses say that recently he'd changed.'

'How can we know what goes through the mind of these migrants?' Panzani echoed his superior. 'Crossing in that way is total folly.'

'It's desperation,' Enrico shifted his weight on the chair. 'When someone is that desperate, they grasp any chance they can.'

'Rossi. This case is closed. It's death by drowning, probable suicide. The autopsy result is irrefutable. And this is the *Questore*'s decision.'

'I'm not denying that he drowned, but it's just not believable that it was suicide.' Despite trying to keep calm, his voice rose.

'And what do you base this on, Rossi?' Panzani leant forward on the *Commissario*'s desk.

Enrico scoffed. It was clear that Panzani only wanted to ingratiate himself with their boss. 'Can we trust the witnesses? He could have been pushed in.'

'Rossi!' Giordano looked over his halfmoon lenses resting on his aquiline nose.

He dropped his head like a bull and stared at Enrico. 'Maybe we haven't understood each other. Ten months. Don't make up a case of homicide ten months from my retirement, just because you want a promotion. We have the coroner's report. So-' Giordano dropped the folder and banged his hand on its cover. 'Suicide. Case closed.'

'It changes nothing for this migrant. He's dead now.' Panzani looked at Enrico slyly. 'In the order of things, does it really matter?'

'It matters. It's a question of justice, no matter who they are, wherever they're from.' Enrico rose from his chair.

'Rossi, if you get between me and a glorious conclusion to my career, I'll make sure you'll be photocopying for the rest of time!' Giordano placed the folder on the heap of documents piled on the side of the desk.

'This damn town is descending into the Wild West. As soon as the shop lights are turned off, people scuttle home. These migrants, they shouldn't even touch alcohol, yet they get drunk, roam the streets and cause mayhem. In the last few months there has been a rash of muggings and assaults. *These* crimes need to be dealt with. We've got to get on top of the situation. Business owners, citizens, people are angry, the mayor wants re-election, the *Questore*, everyone is breathing down my neck. And what are we doing? We're inventing a case of homicide!' Giordano had become irritated.

Panzani broke the silence. 'I agree. The situation is intolerable. This is all because of the frigging Dublin Regulation. Migrants don't want to be registered in Italy, otherwise they'll be stuck. They want to be in France or Germany, so they'd rather dodge the authorities and rest up in that makeshift camp under the fly-over and wait for a chance to get over the border.'

'See, Rossi? Panzani's got the point. We're being overwhelmed because *Monsieur le Président* has closed the border despite Schengen. That's just what I needed between me and my retirement!' Giordano waved his desk calendar in the air, then composed himself.

Corsica. Enrico knew that Giordano had nothing else on his mind. He could imagine in ten months' time, Giordano would pack up his things with the alacrity and agility of a thief and be off. The coffee machine on the bookcase caught Enrico's attention. Giordano refused to drink the foul liquid that poured out of the vending machine downstairs. Since its appearance, Panzani had stopped knocking on Giordano's door with his idiotic grin and a cup of unrequested coffee in hand. Enrico was aware that that scheming two-faced bastard Panzani, with whom he still had to work, would pounce on the tiniest mistake to get above him.

'So, Rossi, understood?'

'Understood. Perfectly well.' Enrico articulated his words slowly.

Giordano took off his glasses and put them on his desk. 'Now go.' His hand pointed to the door and waved, shooing them out.

Enrico's attention fell on Giordano's reading glasses. He knew that *Commissario* never wore them around his neck. He wasn't a man to wear chains. Chains, he put on others.

'Justice, Enrico?' Panzani pulled out his binoculars from the case, wound down the window and started to scan.

Enrico had parked the unmarked police car not far from the fly-over where migrants had camped.

'And maybe with a capital J?' added Panzani.

'How can Giordano consider it a glorious end to his career?' Enrico's jaw stiffened as soon as he let slip his thoughts. His mind hadn't stopped grinding with anger since leaving Giordano's office.

'You slammed the door pretty forcefully.' Panzani peered around the binoculars and looked at Enrico. 'And now you want to find Yousouf's sister, Yasmina?' Panzani returned to watch the camp. 'Although the case is closed.'

Enrico remained silent.

'These here are the ones who are ducking identification. How the hell can they live like this? Out in the open, in winter. Look. Broken supermarket trolleys, crates, plastic bags, litter everywhere. There's even a knackered pushchair. What's it for? There are no children. What a dump! Someone has stretched out a cord to hang their shirts.' Panzani swung his binoculars further around. 'And that van?'

A Transit had just come to a stop. Two people got out and opened up the back.

'Those are volunteers who work with the priest, Don Paolo, to help the migrants.' Enrico watched the young man and woman as they started dishing out hot food. 'There are still people who are compassionate and care for others.'

Enrico observed the queue that had formed at the back of the van. Young men, dark skinned, heads bent seemingly under the weight of their hoods, in reality bowed by the burden of their long journey.

'We should identify those volunteers!'

'Don't talk bullshit! They're helping.' Enrico turned towards his colleague. 'You know bloody well that these poor souls had a terrible time getting here. They've been exploited by the traffickers, have been loaded onto unseaworthy boats and have risked their lives to get to Lampedusa. These are the ones who survived. Now they're in limbo here, hoping to get across the border. They've got nothing.'

'Yousouf's sister definitely won't be here,' said Panzani. 'It's just men.' He put down his binoculars. 'How are you so sure that your migrant was murdered? Has his sister talked you into believing it?' Panzani returned to his binoculars and looked out again. 'Maybe she's promised you a fuck, if you poke around for her. Jesus! If we had to find murderers to get laid, we'd all end up like Don Paolo,' Panzani switched to a shrill, 'speaking with an angelic voice.'

Enrico continued watching the volunteers as they dispensed food.

'But then, Rossi,' – Panzani lowered his binoculars – 'where would you take her? To your bedroom when your mother is out shopping? As I told you, you can always use my studio flat at the weekends when I'm in Genoa. Whenever and with whoever.' Panzani lifted the lenses again.

'I told you before, I'm not interested.'

'But then, if you do her, you'll have to marry her, she's a Muslim. Have you thought what that would do to your mother? She'd have a stroke. Now, that would be the perfect murder. You, of all people –'

'Shut the fuck up!' Enrico started the engine. The car jolted forward. He heard the thud of the binoculars smacking Panzani in the face.

The car wheels growled on the track, raising dust in the air.

SHEENA COOK

Sheena Cook grew up on a farm in Scotland, became a lawyer, then did an MFA in creative writing at Bennington, Vermont. Two sections of this novel were chosen by Ian Rankin and Louise Welsh for Scottish Arts Trust awards. Sheena's interested in exploring suppressed generational rage and its awakening.

smjcook@mac.com

Men Would Kill For This

The opening of a novel

SEPTEMBER

'This is delicate,' my father's lawyer said, on the phone.

'If you're phoning to tell me again that my brother's getting the whole farm, that farmers' daughters get shafted, seriously, it's not news.' In the years since my traineeship with her, I had forgotten a lot of what she had taught me, but never this.

'That's not what I'm phoning to tell you,' the lawyer said.

I sat on the shepherd hut's wall, or what remained of it. 'It's fine. Dad wanted the farm to stay intact. Best way was leave it to the boy. Girls can marry farmers, not *be* farmers.'

'Iris, stop. Your father was supposed to come in and sign a new will. He had an appointment on Monday morning, but he had his — his accident.'

Accident, we're calling it. I see.

'Obviously, the new will isn't signed, but he made the amendments in his own handwriting in his old will. As you know, if those amendments are in ink, initialed, dated and witnessed, they're valid.'

'What's the point? Benjamin will get the farm.'

'That IS the point. Your father's new will changed that.'

'I don't get it.'

'He changed his will to leave the farm equally to both you and Benjamin. You get your share of the farm after all. But only if we get the original document. Can you get into the house? If we can't find it, we have to stick with the terms of the original signed will I have here, the one that obviously favours your brother. Your father told me he changed the safe combination and gave it to you.'

The envelope with the new combination Dad had given me was in my pocket, but my brother had locked the farmhouse after Dad died. I would have to find a way in.

I walked in my wellingtons from the shepherd's hut to the farmhouse. The day before, I had moved into the caravan Dad had put beside the shepherd's hut. He had been right, I wanted it. Not only that, I loved it, the silence of it; an uncultivated part of the farm where nobody went.

As I passed the well by the bog park, I had to glance away. Our own, spring-fed well water with its troublesome pump. Sweet water straight from deep in the earth to our taps. I drank bottled water everywhere else I went. It was difficult to explain the sweetness of home water: spring grass and watery blue skies with an undertone of silage.

We wouldn't be able to use the well now. Not for a while.

My father had still lived in my childhood home, which had also been his childhood home; a stone farmhouse beside a steading where he kept cattle and sheep and a few pigs. He grew his own cabbage and kale and potatoes, and made his oatmeal brose with the pale green kale broth. He hardly watched television. He preferred to sit in the evenings beside the fire in the lamplight with a book of poetry and a teacup of whisky.

Now, I stood behind the steading, and took a sip of the last of Dad's Laphroaig from his hip flask to mask the smell of silage.

Yesterday, the day after my father died, my brother sent me a text: *never come near the farm, never contact me again, I've had enough.*

When I tried to phone, then text him, it became clear he had blocked my number.

Someone tapped me on the shoulder. I jumped. It was George the pigman. He had the knack of appearing from nowhere, probably from a lifetime of working quietly with animals.

'I suppose it's all his now,' he said.

'That's what I've been told,' I said, stepping in mud.

'Should have been yours,' he said. 'You were the one up to your oxters in sharny dubs.'

George was possibly mocking me with his use of our local dialect, suspecting I had forgotten the words. I'd been gone a long time but not long enough to lose my childhood language.

And he was right. I was often outside covered in stinky mud up to my underarms following him about the fields and muddy backroads. Over his shoulder, I caught sight of yellow pages hung on a string for toilet roll in the outside loo, or chunty as we used to call it. The smell of diesel came from the shed where tractors went to die.

'Do you know where my brother is?' I asked. I didn't particularly want to bump into him.

George pointed to the field furthest from the house.

'He's fixing a combine. Joyce brought him a fine piece for his fly. He'll be up there 'til lousin' time.'

If Joyce had brought some of her home baking for my brother's afternoon tea, he would be gone until lousin' time or the end of the workday. I had an hour.

Joyce was George's wife and now my brother's housekeeper. Joyce knew everything about us. When we were little, she was my mother's home help, had changed our nappies, pulled splinters from our hands, threatened a skelpit dowp but never laid a hand on us. It was Joyce's ample body in her crossover pinny I fled to whenever my mother raged. If anyone had asked me to choose my punishment, I would have picked Joyce's skelpit doup over my mother's jolly good walloping about the ears any day.

George shambled off to the steading's far side, and I turned to go into the house.

My brother hopefully wouldn't have told George he had forbidden me from crossing the threshold.

But Joyce was jogging towards me from up the hill, a basket on her arm. She flung her ankles out to the side as she ran, each making a glorious semi-circle from the knee down.

'Long time, no see, stranger,' she shouted. 'I heard you were back, so I made you a quick flycup. Come and give me your news.'

This was going to cut into my time inside the house. Joyce could talk. We sat on the recumbent stone outside the kitchen window. How it got there was a mystery, and it was too big to haul away, but it was a handy spot to sit in the sunshine if you didn't want visitors in over the threshold. Joyce poured tea from a flask and handed me a piece of her lemon curd roly-poly, still warm.

'Are you okay?' she said.

God no, I wasn't okay at all. But, for the purposes of this conversation, I said, 'I'm fine.'

'Your brother's had a difficult time of it,' she said.

And the rest of us haven't? To stop myself saying that, I put some roly-poly in my mouth.

'Benjamin expecting you, is he?'

'Yes. Yes, he is. He asked me to meet him to talk about the will.' I lied to her for the first time that day, and I liked it. It tasted good on my tongue, better than roly-poly. Shame that I was about to break into my own father's house to steal a document made me lie. And rage that my brother assumed that the farm, the gooseberries in the garden, the house, its contents, the shepherd's hut, my caravan, were already his. And that he had possibly got it wrong, and now that our father was out of the way, someone had to take a stand and that someone was me.

Or maybe it was fear. I wouldn't admit this to Joyce, but I was frightened of my brother. I had seen tenderness come from him, but I had also seen violence, and it was difficult to know which circumstance would produce which response. But my body knew the source of my fear.

My phone buzzed with a text from the lawyer: *Are you in the house yet? Have you found it?*

Tea with the pigman's wife, I texted back.

We need it soon, came the reply.

I had experience with lengthy, Joyce-caused delays.

'So you've come home to your trees,' Joyce said. 'They say you're happiest among the trees you grew up with, the ones you played under as a child. And here they are. Your pine trees, your silver birch, your walnut.'

'Possibly not mine anymore.'

Neither of us spoke while we each tried to get used to the implications.

'It doesn't matter who your father was,' Joyce said, in one of her glorious non-sequiturs. 'It matters who you remember he was.'

'What do you mean, who he was?'

'Oh, I see, you don't know.'

'Don't know what?' I couldn't finish the roly-poly.

'I'm sorry,' she said, 'not my story to tell, but I suppose it'll come out now.'

I waited for more. Perhaps she was staying silent to keep the peace. Silence was more powerful than language on our farm. She clearly wasn't going to say any more, so I said goodbye, walked over the grass and pulled an apple from the tree. It shook raindrops onto my face. Most apples had fallen, wasting their sweetness on the ground. I stepped in a puddle and water seeped into my boot. The rubber must have withered in the years since I had worn them. Cold, damp. Into your wellie, through your socks, freezing and turning into chilblains. God how I hated a childhood of cold feet. But the farmhouse was warmer inside now, wasn't it?

I knocked at the back door and waited on the doorstep.

The old roses, heads heavy with rain, clung to the wall, honeysuckle strangling them now. Damp leaves had collected under the drainpipe where the sun never shone. I peered into the playroom window over the deep windowsill as a distant tractor started up and dieseled away.

I tried the back door handle. It was locked.

When I was about seven years old, and my brother six, he sat on the windowsill, emptied my navy leather pencil case, and poured a whole bottle of white pills into it. He took a rolling pin from the kitchen and crushed the pills the way he'd seen Mother do to a bag of digestive biscuits for a cheesecake base. He told me he had made a sherbet fountain, and I was to eat it with a teaspoon. The game was to do as he said, so I did. I didn't know what I was eating. It was gritty and sour, but fizzy like sherbet, so I persevered.

Mother happened into the playroom and saw the empty aspirin bottle and the white powder around my mouth. The overdose might have been fatal, but she didn't call an ambulance. Instead, she took the time to change me from farm clothes into my pink Sunday cardigan and white frilly Sunday pants, so the hospital people wouldn't think we were slovenly. On the airing cupboard floor were three tins: one for dusters, one for shoe polish and one for Sunday pants, so the pants smelled of shoe polish and dusters.

Dad got called home from his tractor to drive me to hospital to get my stomach pumped. My brother stood on the doorstep and waved us away, smiling, job done.

Now, inside the old cowshed, bundles of rusty keys on bailer twine hung on nails driven into the stone wall. I took down a bundle and went back to the farmhouse door. I tried key after key, until one worked. I pushed the door open, and a faint smell of Dad's cigars and woodsmoke came at me from inside.

In the old days, I would have been offered a mug of coffee and some home bakes. There were always home bakes in a farmhouse; fruit scones, or tiffin cake — chocolatey boys, as Dad had called them. I'd always be invited in.

I shouted and nobody came, so I walked through the cloakroom filled with wellies in various staging of perishing, into the kitchen over the old blue linoleum, curling at the corners now, begging us to lift it and take a peek underneath.

Time moves slowly after a death. It takes seven days for a soul to leave the body, and I wanted to be there when it happened. I hadn't been with my dad when he died, and this distressed me more than anything. He died alone, no hand squeezing his, no one leaning in to hear his last whisper, what he wanted to say at the end. I needed to know what his last whisper was, because now we had a shambles.

I wanted a thorough wander to see if I could find the answer to fix this.

The air inside the farmhouse was still. Life inside it had stopped, and the house couldn't breathe until the next chapter of its life could begin. I paced the house, avoiding the room I had to go into.

I rifled through papers on the kitchen counter, his diary beside the phone. He kept it open, so anyone could read it. It meant he didn't have to tell people where he was. We could simply walk into the kitchen and check his diary. The last few days were blank, but a few days ago, he had written, 'Into town, sign doc at lawyers.'

And of course, he never made it.

I didn't open those awkward cupboards above the fridge. I couldn't reach them without a step stool. No time for now.

The music on the piano was bleached from lying in the sun, another sheet was marked in circles by a vase of water. No time to sit and play the Schubert my brother was never able to learn.

I rumbled through the box of cufflinks in Dad's bedroom, held his pillowcase to my face, sprayed some of his Old Spice aftershave onto my wrist, picked up his bristly hairbrush. Felt inside the pockets of all his jackets hanging in the wardrobe, all the while listening for my brother's Land Rover.

In the pockets, I found painkillers, sticky plasters and tissues with spots of blood on them. So many tissues, so many spots of blood. He had been hiding how bad his illness had become from us all.

I put my head around the door of my childhood bedroom. Still the old candlewick bedspread with its hairy caterpillars marching across it. And the secret box room filled with my grandmother's letters.

No rooms left to pillage apart from his study. I opened the door quietly so as not to disturb him. He was peaceful in there, in his coffin lined with lilac silk, hands folded, resting on his chest, in a pose he would never have made while he was alive. There should be a cigar in one hand and a whisky in a crystal tumbler as he told a story he found far funnier than the rest of us. His cheeks were sunken now, giving him a severe look. The undertaker had done a good job with the cover-up. You'd never know about the fall. He'd left the dark bruises on the backs of his hands though — those were from his normal illness.

At least he had his party kilt on, his Dress Gordon with its dandified and daring raspberry stripe and his black kilt jacket for dinners, dancing and funerals (his everyday green tweed one hung in his wardrobe for his grandsons) and his cream wool kilt socks, knitted by Mrs. Donaldson in the village before she lost her mind. She had knocked on the door before Dad died and told me on the doorstep she had had a vision: Dad had come to her and told her he wanted to be buried in his dress kilt. 'You'll always be his favourite,' she'd say to me if I bumped into her in the village over the years when I came home for a visit. 'He sees a lot of himself in you.' I loved hearing this and glowed from inside, but now I wondered why, while he was alive and had the chance, did he never give me the tiniest indication.

I'd phoned the undertaker to tell him to put Dad into his full kilt because losing him had turned us all superstitious. No one wanted to displease him or the gods and goddesses of the underworld or the overworld. Now, he was dressed for dancing wherever he was going. And his skean dhu down the side of his sock and red flashings at the tops of his socks and his good sporran. And, incongruously, we kept him in his lilac shirt to match the silk coffin lining. Why an undertaker would choose lilac for a farmer was beyond me.

'Sorry, Dad,' I said, putting the back of my finger to his beloved cheekbone, 'I have to do this.'

I kneeled in front of the antiquated safe, pulled the crinkled envelope from my pocket, dialed in the numbers and turned the massive circular handle in the same way we learned to do when we were little.

JUNE
Three months earlier

Our farm never made more than a subsistence living, but its soil yielded small new potatoes with the flavour of hazelnuts, the same as when I was young. Every year I went home for the first digging, eating them with melting salted butter on a June evening after the rain.

At around the same time came the first raspberries. My father had planted those fruit bushes among his beehives, and tended them wearing a tweed suit, trousers held up with orange baler twine, his wool undershirt open at the neck, fixing tractors, stopping to write notes for poems with a pencil into his pocket-sized hardback notebook, until he could be alone at his roll top desk.

On the first Sunday in June, I drove home. After a couple of hours on the road, the countryside grew familiar. I was back inside the boundary of my home hills. It was late afternoon, and the sun was low. The same early summer light as when I used to get off the bus after school with my brother.

I turned into the lane that curved towards home, with trees on either side and grass growing up the middle. It tickled the car's underbelly. There was room for only one car. If another came towards me, I would either have to reverse back to the lane's entrance or stop in the layby at my brother's cottage.

I climbed out of the car to open the top gate and take a breath of sweet farm air. The road ran down Lindsayhill towards the farm and all it contained: the scent of my grandmother's pink roses around the kitchen window; the view over barley fields to the top road with the red postie's van coming through in bursts along the hedges; muddy back roads with great puddles to cycle through.

I pressed my hand into the pillowy sphagnum moss growing on the top of the dry stone dyke. We used to sit on these mossy walls on breaks between roguing barley. I never had any idea why it was called that, when all we were doing was pulling stray stalks of wild oats from the fields.

Soft rain soaked my hair, eyelashes and lips. It wasn't proper rain but thin mist wetter than rain. It soaked the beech trees my grandfather had planted, knowing he wouldn't get the good of their shade.

My father was sitting on the doorstep in the open doorway drinking tea – a round butter biscuit spread with treacle in his other hand, possibly waiting for me, possibly not.

But the potatoes weren't ready. That day, he dug some up and said they were green. 'You'll have to stay a few more days,' he said. 'Sunday. We'll have them next Sunday.'

I sat at the kitchen table, and he brought scrambled eggs on toast, the buttery kind only he made. He tucked a tea towel under his chin and ate a bowl of raspberries, one by one, dipping each with his teaspoon into a saucer of cream, letting the ivory liquid fall from the berry back into the bowl.

My father kept most of his thoughts and feelings to himself, economical with his words, as if they might be taxed. His sentences ended unexpectedly. I waited for more, but more never came. I'd learned to pay attention to the unsaid, to what lay between his words.

We had a secret language though; a mash-up of lines from others' poems.

He held the last raspberry high, letting the remaining cream fall. 'As the poets said, so much depends on this, upon a red raspberry dipped in white cream falling into the bowl. Men would kill for this.'

I spent the week there, walking the bumpy roads of my childhood and sitting in the kitchen rocking chair beside the old piano, letting the rhythm of the farm, where time collapsed, pass at the right speed. The postman came on his bike in the middle of weekday mornings in time for elevenses; the grocer in his van on Tuesday morning with a tin of custard and pinhead oats for my father's brose; the fish man on Wednesday with lemon sole or herring for the fridge and a piece of salmon skin tossed to the blind cat; the cleaning lady on Thursday; the butcher's van on Friday with a couple of sausages or a pork chop and a few slices of black pudding, and the baker on Friday afternoon with a lemon tart, floury baps and oatcakes for the larder.

There was only time on the farm, where the best of life was lived quietly, where nothing happened but a calm journey through the day, where change was imperceptible and precious life was everything.

I spent the evenings playing the old piano. It was exactly as I left it – the open book of Chopin preludes, the old vase on top.

He had wanted me, his only daughter, to get off the farm and go to university, so he sold the pictures off his walls, his mother's silver from the drawers and the cattle from the field. I was sent away to learn Latin and French while he sat on his proud combine harvester, cutting barley.

My brother stayed, moved into the cottar house, and waited for his turn to move into the farmhouse, which wouldn't happen before my father's death.

We spent my last morning making a batch of jam from the raspberry bushes outside the kitchen window. He stirred the pot on the Rayburn while the red liquid bubbled. I sterilised the jam jars. His hand shook as he ladled in the jam, and I wiped the sides of the jars with my mother's old dishcloth. I held the cellophane covers on top of each jar as he stretched a rubber band over them. We lined the glass jars full of scarlet liquid on the larder shelves, more than enough for all the coming summer's and winter's teas.

The first new potatoes from the garden were ready, so my father poured a scull of them covered in earth into the red plastic basin in the sink. He had been right, they needed seven more days. We stood under raindrops falling on the skylight, cleaning the potatoes, my father's head bent towards mine. His old hands were better suited to fixing broken tractor axles than cleaning small potatoes. He let each badly cleaned potato fall with a splash into the basin. The purple bruises on the backs of his arms made a ghost hand reach through my ribs and squeeze my heart.

I boiled the potatoes and brought them to the table. He dipped potatoes one by one into a ramekin of melted butter and let it drip off, the same as he had done with the raspberries. 'Everything,' he said, 'depends upon this.'

Later, I joined my father for his walk. The long evening waved yellow with broom, and the air was thick with the coconut scent of it. The sun sank over the river, and he talked about the golden light with wonder, seeing it for the first time, or the last.

He stopped to rebuild the fallen stones of our neighbour's dry stone dyke. That's what people did there, they stopped to fix broken things, averting someone's pain before it happened. There was no need for the neighbour to know his dry stone dyke had been falling. Any one of my father's neighbours would do the same for him. It gave me a secure feeling, of people moving about their days, silently watching out for each other, helping the earth go around.

He walked bent forward looking at the ground, hands clasped behind his back, carrying his losses in the muscles around his spine. 'The clock,' he said, 'only ticks one way.'

We walked through the sunshine and grass into the outshift, where the fields frayed into the trees of my far-off childhood, the swallows showing us the way. We walked through the fields along the dry stone dykes covered with spongy moss. The peasie-wits dove into the yellow broom, and white butterflies landed among the daisies and folded their wings for a rest. I walked with my father into the twilight, the wolf light, the time when the familiar became wild.

'Life is long,' he said 'but not if you like it. If you like it, it's short.'

We reached the clearing in the woods where the shepherd's hut stood, which had seemed to me a dappled church. I used to come here when I was little to find my father, picking my way through dark patches of spilled diesel on the ground, past broken tractors drowning in nettles, along the bumpy road to the well, then down among the trees at the bog park.

We sat now inside the shepherd's hut, left to moulder. Decay had made progress since I was last there, the walls now so long fallen that moss had enveloped the stones. The red table I'd dragged there still sat between two tree stumps.

He told me he was leaving me this shepherd's hut. He would park a caravan beside it so I could live there while I renovated it. 'You'll want it soon.'

I had no idea what he meant.

'The doctor told me it's bone marrow cancer,' he said, out of nowhere. 'If you're lucky to survive it, you get acute leukemia.'

That ghost hand dug its nails into my heart. I waited for him to say more, but he didn't.

He turned to the red table and put his palms flat on it, as if he could no longer bear his own weight. He searched my face. He was either examining me for a reaction or pleading for help. I waited.

He lowered his head, taking a moment to listen to his heart and find the right words. 'It's a richt scunner,' he said, using one of his usual understatements. His sentences contained fewer words than necessary, every other word unspoken, so I never knew if he meant one thing or another. He could have meant becoming ill was a scunner or having hands too awkward to scrub small potatoes or ladle jam into jars was a scunner.

In the middle of the silence, before I could ask how long he had left, he walked away.

Back at home, I lit the stove with the winter's last store of wood, arranged a bowl of sweet peas on a tray, made a pot of tea and spread my father's favourite treacle on an Orkney oatcake as we sat in the sitting room on the sofa, resting our feet on the wooden table. The logs burned in the stove, scenting the air with woodsmoke as wind gusted around us outside and rain hurled itself at the windowpanes. The poetry volumes packed onto the shelves above our heads would not be consulted tonight.

I sat with him while we gave each other time to work out how ill he was, and I pictured him alone in the farmhouse by the fire, pretending not to need help, not wanting to cause a fuss by phoning the doctor to ask for a home visit. What would happen when he could no longer drive? If he fell in the night, lying quietly in pain on the flagstone floor in his pyjamas, who would he cry out to? The hand tightened around my heart. I looked out to my brother's cottage as his kitchen light went out.

'We'll get a nurse in during the night,' I said, 'and I'll come up at weekends and as often as I can.'

He pulled an old envelope from a pile of papers and wrote some numbers in his shaky handwriting. 'New safe combination. Keep it,' he said. 'You'll need it.'

It was a set of numbers: 140923. The safe combination since we were little had been his date of birth. This was different. I didn't think much of it at the time. I simply shoved the envelope into my pocket.

I said it was time to stop hauling himself underneath tractors to fix them, pay for a farm manager instead, and sit in his deck chair in the garden with the sun on his face and the breeze in his hair, listening to the shipping forecast on the radio warning about gales losing their identity over the Atlantic until the end of his days. But we both knew he wouldn't. He would sit on his beloved tractor until his last day.

BENJAMIN DAVIES

Benjamin Davies trained at the Drama Centre London and won an Olivier Award for his acting work. He relocated to the United States where he lived for many years. His first novel, *They Moved Away the Highway*, is a neo-noir thriller set in Los Angeles and explores the dark roads we travel when pushed to extremes.

bendavies37@gmail.com
www.bendavieswriter.com

They Moved Away the Highway

The opening of a novel

PROLOGUE
Salta Verde Point, 2019

The force of the explosion threw her to the ground. She was blinded by the flash of light, her face warm from the heat. She wanted to call out but couldn't risk alerting him to her presence. If only she was surrounded by law enforcement. But she was alone with no legal jurisdiction. For the first time in her career, she didn't care about the court room. About evidence. What she could or could not prove. That's if this ever went to trial. But if he won today, she would become a missing person. She knew there was no such thing as closure. Only justice. She was willing to do whatever it took to stop him.

Inland the sky was darker. She managed to get to her feet and took cover behind a eucalyptus, but her balance was off. Peeking from behind the tree, she saw the cabin in flames. Wood, debris, and branches burning. Turning towards the sea, she could taste the salt. The light was almost gone when she made for the cliffs. The ground, wet. She began to speed up, fighting the storm's winds.

Closer to the cliff's edge, she saw the warm glow of a boat, rising and falling in the water. She hid next to some fern bushes. She needed to get down to the beach and onto the boat. The adrenaline was still pumping, making her dizzy.

Something was wrong with her hearing. Her ear was full of a sloshing static sound, like a drowning shortwave radio. She wiped the fluid out of her ear, then inspected her fingers. It was blood. Normal sounds like the wind became abstract, scratchy, and painful.

Then it stopped. She heard a twig snap behind her. Someone was there. Breathing heavily. She could smell smoke. Maybe she should jump off the cliff into the water. What if she didn't make it? She was trapped. She was about to scream when a hand covered her mouth.

CHAPTER ONE – WILLIAM RAINE
Catalina Island, 1999

William felt the reverberations when the book slammed shut. He watched birds fly by in the distance. High up on the cliffs it had been quiet, the clouds floated along, and the ocean was still. William was used to the city; he couldn't stand the silence. To him the loud noise was welcome, even though Joseph's anger was not. He looked at the thirty-two-year-old man, who placed the old book back into his rucksack. The air up here was so fresh. Joseph stank of the streets; his hair was matted and had become dreadlocked. Stale sweat filled the air around him. William hoped that when he was Joseph's age he would be in much better condition. He had thirteen years to improve his circumstances, but at least he already smelled better.

William put his own bag down. 'Are you happy now?'

Joseph turned. Stared at William. He looked back out at the ocean.

William cleared his throat. 'I think it was an orca's fin before.'

Joseph didn't take the bait.

He coughed again. 'Maybe they're just rocks that look like a whale.'

Still nothing.

William needed to push a button. 'If you're looking to shoot up or whatever, go for it.'

Joseph looked pissed off as he pulled his rucksack under his legs. 'Don't ever steal my stuff again.'

'You just had to ask, man. I would have given it to you. You didn't need to smash it shut.'

Joseph got to his feet. 'Just because I've been loaning you books doesn't give you the right to take one from my bag!'

William put his hands up in protest. 'Listen, man–'

'No! It's not okay to steal, "man."'

'You said I could borrow any book?' William rolled his eyes.

'It's not my book. It's precious. It belongs to someone else.'

William picked up his backpack. 'All great artists steal. It was stupid. I'm sorry, but really you should say sorry. Because you've been feeding me books, like a drug dealer. Getting me hooked.'

Joseph shook his head.

'It's this.' William pulled out an envelope from his backpack. The wind almost blew it out of his hand. He gestured to rip the envelope in two but didn't.

After a while, the older man spoke. 'Have you opened it?'

'No.'

'You should just open it.' Joseph sat up.

'I can't.' He pulled the flap half-open then passed it to Joseph.

Joseph turned it over in his hands. Examining the college address stamped on the back, he took out the letter and read aloud.

Dear William Raine,
Thank you so much for your interest in The School for Professional Arts.
We really enjoyed meeting you. Unfortunately, the standard is very high this year and we are unable to offer you a place. We know you will feel disheartened by this news but please feel free to apply again next year.
We wish you all the best.
Gloria Brown

The silence went on too long. William didn't look at the trained artist.

'I'm sorry, William. You, okay? You're welcome to apply next year.'

William shook his head. He seemed to be listening to something that wasn't there. A song he didn't like was being played in his head, over and over again. He felt smaller than Joseph, even though the other man was sitting down.

'When I went there ten years ago, Gloria was in my class. Can't believe she's running the course now. William, I agree with her, you're nineteen. I didn't do that course until I was twenty-two. There's no shame in reapplying. It shows you really want it. They like that.'

'What would be the point?' He looked out at the sea.

'It's just a year.'

'I need to go this year, man.' He finally looked at Joseph. 'I need to go.'

'Why?'

William was crestfallen. Something was going on behind his eyes. All that came out of his mouth was, 'I just do.' It was like he had lost everything.

'If it's your mom… Understand, she wants the best for you. Apply next year.'

'Fuck you!'

'What?'

'What if your friend Gloria refuses me entry next year?'

Joseph stayed sitting on the floor. 'Why do you even want to be an artist? It's a road of pain.'

William looked at Joseph and thought he looked older than thirty-two. He had these lines under his eyes. If he was a car he would have had high mileage. It wasn't just the drugs. It was something else driving him. 'You don't think I'm good enough, do you?'

Joseph shook his head. 'I didn't say that. I wouldn't recommend anyone do it.'

'You did it.'

'I had no choice.' He threw his arms up.

'Because you're a good artist.'

'If you need to do something you have no choice, and you'll do it whatever anyone says.'

Joseph looked homeless there on the ground. What had William been thinking? He had been seduced by the artwork but look who made it. A broken man. He talked a good game about art school and the pure struggle wasn't a waste, but he looked wasted as a person. William believed he could be a great artist. What could an art school really teach him?

Joseph was a good painter but wasn't successful. Now all his Jim Morrison shine withered and died right there in the dust. Before this moment William thought Joseph was a good role model, but maybe he was just a junkie. An older guy with a drug problem who had wanted to get close to William's mom and play dad for a while. Joseph told William he brought him here to get him out of the city but now William wanted to get as far away from Joseph as possible. William almost felt sorry for him.

'Fuck it. Maybe I could travel.'

'Travel in your mind - that's why I've been lending you the books. Maybe I could sell you one book.'

William moved away from him. Stood a foot from the sheer drop of the cliff and looked at the rocks below. 'Who are they to tell me I'm no good?'

'Forget it. Which book do you want to buy?'

William looked over his shoulder. Joseph in the dirt holding old books. He didn't want any of those. He wanted the one Joseph refused to sell. 'No. You know which one.' Then, he turned back and spat on the rocks below.

'I can't. Pick another. *The Structure of Magic* or *The Celestine Prophecy*. Maybe *Diary of a Drug Fiend* or *Thus Spoke Zarathustra*?'

William couldn't look at him so he sat on the cliff edge. Letting his legs hang over the drop. He knew Joseph didn't like heights; he wasn't moving from where he sat. William wanted to test him. 'Why not *The Lesser Key of Solomon*?'

Joseph looked pale. 'I can't. I could do *Thus Spoke Zarathustra*. Twenty bucks? Or you can just have it.'

'I've read it.' He decided to raise the stakes, holding onto the edge, William turned to face Joseph whilst hanging his legs off the cliff edge. 'From chaos comes order. But does order generate chaos?'

Joseph looked scared. 'Good question.'

William slipped down hanging by his fingertips. 'What's wrong?'

'Pull yourself up, now.' Joseph offered him a hand.

'I won't fall.' He grabbed Joseph's hand and pulled his arm. 'Do you believe in fate?'

Joseph yanked William up and away from the drop. 'Sit back here for a bit.'

They sat next to each other looking out to the ocean.

'Listen, to me, ten years goes quick. Art school is expensive. When I was on the course, I got a scholarship.'

'Yeah, look what good it did you.'

'What does that mean?'

'Sorry, man, you are, you're a good artist, but you just get high all the time.'

'It's part of the process.'

'Maybe that could be your first art book. *The Process of Being an Addict* by Joseph Caplan. You could take different drugs, paint the same picture and people could guess what drugs you were on.'

Joseph tensed up. 'You're really testing me today. I'm going to let that one slide.'

'Whatever.' William found a stone and threw it over the edge.

'Show some respect. Did you speak to Gloria like that in your interview? People don't generally want to work with assholes.'

'She probably thinks I'm a junkie like you. That's why she didn't offer me a place.'

'You're a thief.'

'Coming from a liar like you, that means a lot.'

'What have I lied about?'

'*The Lesser Key of Solomon*. Where did it come from?'

Joseph paused then said. 'I borrowed it.'

'Who from?' William had him on the back foot.

'It doesn't matter.' Joseph put his rucksack on.

'You're going to beg me to buy that book when you run out of money. Junkie prick.'

Joseph raised his arm to strike, but stopped himself.

'Finally. Just like my dad! That's why mom would never date you. She doesn't like being a punch bag.' William shuffled away from him.

'Watch your mouth. I was trying to help you. You can tell your mom that. It's more than most.' The gap between them grew as he edged away from William.

'Bullshit. You want a charity case so you can feel better about your own life.' William got up and stood by the edge.

Joseph took a breath. 'Look. I shouldn't have said what I said. I'm sorry.'

'Why?'

'I don't want you to fall.'

'Yeah, you do. Then you can whisper into my mother's ear. "I'm sorry the charity case is dead, but I could stay over?"

'I don't think you're a charity case. I was just upset.'

William backed away from the edge and sat a meter away from Joseph.

'Let's have a smoke.'

'I'm not into that.' William looked around in the dirt for a rock.

'It's just weed.'

'Nah.'

Joseph took off his bag. He searched for a book and a glass pipe. 'I'll give you my copy of Zarathustra.'

'Thanks. I wonder who owns *The Lesser Key of Solomon*?'

'A friend.' Joseph put something in the glass pipe and smoked it. Inhaling deep. It acted fast. His shoulders dropped and body relaxed. He lit it again.

They didn't speak for a while.

Joseph slouched against a rock. He was really high.

William smiled and joined him. Through the ferns he could see the red warning sign for the cliff edge. 'I know who lent you the book.'

'What?' Joseph tried to sit up, but he was sedated.

William put his arm around Joseph and gave him a little hug. He managed to slide his arms around Joseph's neck, creating a sleeper hold.

'Get off me!' Joseph struggled and tried to elbow the younger man.

William pulled tighter.

Joseph tried to force William's arm out from under his jaw.

William squeezed Joseph's neck as tight as he could.

Joseph began to lose consciousness. After a while his body went limp.

William released his hold on Joseph's neck. He peered over the cliff's edge. Pulling Joseph's rucksack over and turning out its contents, William found '*The Lesser Key of Solomon*'. It was an expensive-looking black book. Then he stuffed everything back into the rucksack and placed the black book into his own backpack.

He sat Joseph's body up and dragged him over to the cliff edge. He let Joseph's legs flop over the drop while he supported his body. Gradually William rocked Joseph forward, letting gravity take him. Headfirst, Joseph fell through the air. After a few moments William heard a crunch like a watermelon exploding on the ground.

He looked over the edge, willing himself to see Joseph's body. He turned away fast when he couldn't recognize the formless mess on the rocks below. He wanted to get out of there, but found himself looking down again. Joseph's head must have entered his chest cavity because it was nowhere to be seen on the ground. William tried not to throw up.

He emptied Joseph's rucksack and scribbled a note on his drawing pad next to the drug pipe. He jumped the fence leaving the scene. As he passed a red warning sign, he dumped Joseph's empty rucksack underneath, intending it to be found.

William disappeared down the empty trail.

CHAPTER TWO – ANDREA AUERBACH
Los Angeles, 2019

Detective Andrea Auerbach had a situation. The siren and the blue lights usually helped with traffic. However, on days like these the streets were deserted. The sky was black, not normal LA weather. Rain had started with a few drops that morning, but fast turned into a monsoon. She knew Angelinos feared driving in the rain. When the streets were wet, they took their lives in their hands. All the forgotten parts of the city were regurgitated on the avenues, streets and boulevards. Debris, pools of oil, car parts, broken shopping carts, homeless people's ephemera, kids' toys, empty animal crates.

Auerbach lived in Silverlake. Her neighborhood was named after the reservoir. It could hold 795 million gallons; it would be full within hours. Millions of gallons of water would fall on the city after hundreds of days without a drop.

She knew Los Angeles needed water, no one was complaining about that, but when the downpours came, they were biblical.

Recently fires plagued Tinsel Town. Sent from above to cleanse every sinful mile. Now a Seattle-style storm had arrived. Afterwards all eighty-eight cities would be hung out to dry in the Santa Ana breeze. Auerbach knew some of the city's history could never be washed clean.

Fountain Avenue was a mess. She took Gower to De Longpre Avenue all the way to Highland Avenue, then a left on to Sunset Boulevard straight to North Formosa Avenue.

Rain buffeted the side of her Dodge Charger as if it were a boat on the ocean. The rubber on her windshield wipers had split from the metal and was scratching the glass. The sound was intense. Auerbach thought the windscreen might break from the pressure. Thankfully, she had spent time in the Pacific Northwest and was used to driving in bad weather. Now on Sunset, she was fast approaching North Formosa.

Auerbach pulled into the parking lot of The Seventh Veil strip club on the corner of Formosa and Sunset. The rain ran down Formosa Avenue like an angry river washing all the rubbish away. Large palm tree husks were sticking out of a storm drain, blocking one side like dinosaur bones. A swell of water lifted them up and sucked them down into the veins of the city, disappearing until the next husks fell.

A Lincoln Navigator pulled up, blocking her path. Rain pounded off the luxury vehicle. A stripper jumped out and went into the back of The Seventh Veil. The Navigator quickly sped off.

Auerbach didn't want to park outside the property; she didn't want to be seen there. So, she parked in the strip mall car park. She locked her car and crossed to the opposite side of Formosa. She saw a street woman watching her from a doorway. The woman was cradling a child's doll. The rain wouldn't stop. Auerbach looked away and moved fast down North Formosa Avenue, scanning the area for anyone else who had seen her arrive.

New apartment blocks three-storeys high stood where original Hollywood bungalows used to be. One or two bungalows with waterlogged gardens still survived.

Auerbach thought she had done her due diligence. She even knew the properties' history. Two Hansel and Gretel style cottages filled the unit of 1330. Built over one hundred years ago by a British actor who had become Hollywood royalty. His film studios still stood two blocks away on North La Brea Avenue. Built in a similar style during the silent film era.

Nothing lasts in Los Angeles, her grandmother used to say. A ten-million-dollar Chinese restaurant complete with green jade roof, a true landmark. It was the hottest place to be seen in its day, but had just been levelled because a film studio needed a new car park. Auerbach had celebrated her grandmother's birthday there, good memories. Now it was dust. To love Los Angeles is to know its Planning Department is no friend of history, she thought.

The fact 1330 Formosa had been left standing all these years was a miracle. A fake piece of Hollywood's original past, untouched. The landlord told Auerbach many stars had lived in the place over the years. However, she knew that now a crime had been committed, none of that mattered. 1330 Formosa's old reputation was gone, replaced by a new bloodier one, just like that of Spahn Ranch and

Wonderland Avenue.

Auerbach sneaked through the gate, crossing the courtyard of 1330. She passed large trees towering over the Rapunzel turret and gingerbread roof. She kept her head down. Rain bounced off the ground all the way up the steps to the front door, still sealed with yellow police tape. She cut the tape and opened the front door. Closed it quickly behind her. The place was a time capsule; it smelled of the life that used to be there. The stale air was a shadow of the past. Auerbach had raced over here this morning because the landlord was due to decorate the whole unit next week.

This Hansel and Gretel style home was the location of the last case with her partner. Detective Jack Marshall died before she closed the double murder/suicide. The father, Fred Mamerow had 'gone postal,' shooting his wife Karen and daughter Marissa, then hanging himself. Definitely not a fairy tale. The trouble was Jack Marshall's diary had arrived unexpectedly. It came in a box of work-related materials from Marshall's widow. Jack had privately written various suspicions about the Formosa murders which would have died with him if Auerbach hadn't read them in his diary that morning. Unfortunately, the case was officially closed. Pressing her shoulder tight against the front door, it opened with a bang.

CHAPTER THREE – FRANK MALCOM
New York City, 2019

New York City boomed. Sirens filled the air. Frank Malcom left his office for the penultimate time. He couldn't risk a cab. Traffic was locked tight, bumper to bumper. The city, a sweatbox. There was a sense that everything was just about ready to blow up. Steam escaped through a red pipe in the street. The junction of Eighth Avenue and West 40th Street was a hot mess and smelled like one. A warm garbage, dollar pizza whiff, all mixed memorably with car fumes and the sweat of the city. The drains were lined with small but frequent fatbergs. *Insipid Street Cheese* would be the title of NYC's perfume. If you smelt it, you wouldn't forget it, Frank thought.

His last day at work. The sun breaking through the steel curtain which protected the glass walls of the New York Times building. His old office building was a contained architectural explosion. It faced off against the tougher looking Port Authority Transport Terminal, stout and practical.

Frank couldn't trust the subway. Better on foot.

He had ten minutes to get to the top of Rockefeller Plaza for a celebratory cocktail with his agent. A twenty-minute walk, easy. Frank started off double timing his stride, but broke into a run when he was next to Birdland jazz club. He took a right down 45th Street, raced up Sixth Avenue and by the time he got to 50th Street he could feel his back drenched with sweat. His time was almost gone, but he still needed to be sixty-five floors up in the air.

Midtown Manhattan disappeared as Frank got into the elevator. A golden rocket to the moon. His ears popped. Moments later, a bell rang. One of the best city views in the world. All other buildings appeared smaller this high up. A shudder ran up the back of his legs, a wobble. Vertigo focused his mind and his body.

As he entered the dining room, he saw Joanna seated at the bar. He took a breath, wiped his brow, and made his way over to her.

'Joanna. You look wonderful. I'm a ball of sweat. Apologies.' He kissed the side of her face. Joanna blushed. Was it the sweat comment or was he supposed to air kiss? Frank still couldn't be that American.

'Hi Frank. How have you been?' She kept eye contact then peeked over his shoulder.

'Good.' Frank smiled slightly and looked over his shoulder to follow her gaze. His insides burned. The one face he didn't need to see. Right here. Right now.

Mick Jordan raised a glass to Joanna and Frank. Frank smiled a bemused grin back, toothy, and fake. Why was this happening to him today?

'Is the New Yorker still paying that hacks bar tab?' He signaled the bar tender.

'Frank.' Joanna raised an eyebrow.

'I've just never seen a snake drinking an Old Fashioned before.' He turned away.

'Remember what Oscar Wilde said about critics.' She sat up straight.

'Oscar bloody Wilde had something to say about every bugger.' Frank smiled.

The bartender appeared. 'Good afternoon. How are you both today?' He put down nuts and olives.

'Well, thank you. And you?' Frank tapped the bar top.

'Great. What can I offer you?'

'Martini, Joanna?'

'Sure.' She placed her napkin on her lap and stabbed an olive with a toothpick.

Frank wasn't going to have this catch up spoiled. 'Two Martini's please sir. Hendricks Gin, Noilly Prat, two olives, ice cold, extremely dry. Thank you.' Frank gave a small theatrical bow with his head.

'Of course.' The bartender returned the gesture and walked away.

Frank felt someone tap him on his shoulder. He turned around and Mick Jordan was staring him straight in the eye. Oh God. Here we go.

'Frank, old boy. Can I get you a drink mate?' His mock English accent sounded like Dick Van Dyke. He leered at Joanna, a bit drunk, big smile, pleased with his pronunciation of *mate*.

Be professional. Be professional: he's half cut.

'Mick. For a moment I thought I was in Bethnal Green not the Rainbow Room. How's Mary Poppins, my old mucker?'

Mick Jordan absorbed the jibe and smiled. 'Henry Higgins, old boy.'

'Yes, *Pygmalion*. Enjoying your lunch?' He smiled back, squaring up to Mick.

Joanna looked uncomfortable. Frank backed off a little and Mick Jordan got the message.

'Fair enough. Frank, I did reach out to your fabulous agent here regarding my review, but no response.' Mick looked at Joanna and she stared back.

'Sounds like the perfect response to your review, old boy.' Frank grinned. 'Only kidding, as Oscar Wilde said.' Frank waited a couple of beats. 'Where would we be without critics?'

'Never personal, Frank. Perhaps a more relevant subject matter may help in the future. What's this I hear about *Vanity Fair?*' Mick folded his arms.

'Just doing some work for them.' Frank looked at the ground.

'Wow - the winner of the George Orwell Award sleeping with the enemy.' Mick tapped Frank in the ribs. 'Should have stayed in London old boy. We've corrupted you!' Mick's crocodile smile made Frank's guts burn.

'Coming from you Mick, that means a lot.' Frank rolled his eyes.

Joanna stepped in. 'Mick, of course we appreciate the heads-up. Things are a little busy. However, many other critics are very complimentary of Frank's latest efforts. We feel it's sad that you're not on board. But we'll get over it. Thanks for saying "Hi". All the best to Martha. Look forward to seeing you again soon.'

Joanna was like a ninja; Mick didn't stand a chance. He smiled and walked back to his table, angling his chair slightly towards the window. Joanna had released the pressure valve, but they needed to be careful. Mick made careers. He was also exceptional at burying writers in places no one could find them again. Mick was probably irked that a Brit was encroaching on his backyard. The *Vanity Fair* comment smacked of hypocrisy. But it got under Frank's skin.

'Can I get you anything else?' The bar tender appeared with their drinks.

'Perfect timing, thank you.' Frank went to pass him a card.

'Frank, I'll get these.' Joanna opened her bag.

'I know you're busy. Thanks for making some time. These are on me.' He gave the bartender his card. 'Twenty percent', he said in a low voice.

'Of course. Thank you.'

Frank picked up his drink, 'Cheers!' They both took long sips. The martini hit its mark. Frank's shoulders dropped slightly as the gin sank down his throat. He didn't speak and neither did Joanna. The silence between them only lasted a moment, but the sound of other couples laughing seemed to grow louder.

'To your book.' She raised her glass.

'Yes.' He took a gulp, 'How's it all going?'

It was a lovely environment. A soft bar stool. A nice cocktail. Joanna paused for a moment. Frank saw a glint of something uncomfortable pass through her eyes. Thankfully she had the good grace not to hang on to it.

'Well.' She gave a warm smile and took another sip.

'What did Mick's email say?' Frank sat forward.

'He's obsessed with *Lies in The Heartland*. Thinks it was your best work and doesn't know why you aren't investigating important social stuff like that.'

'That was ten years ago.' Frank smelled brine in the glass as he took another sip.

'I know.' Joanna popped an olive in her mouth.

'It was more than just crime. It was Woodward and Bernstein. They were my gods. It was Old School. I miss that time. Who can be heard over the internet nowadays.'

'Why not try something like that again?' Joanna bit down hard and yelped in pain.

'Are you okay?'

'Stone in the olive.' Joanna looked upset with herself. She took a moment and then took a sip of her drink. 'I'm fine, Frank. I need to go shortly. Why not get the old scent back? Crime never goes out of fashion.'

'Where are you off to?' Frank finished his cocktail.

'Your old stomping ground. London town. Then Paris. Phillipa Mathews' new book launch and her son's wedding. Unity Harper is doing a talk at the Sorbonne then being knighted by the Order of Arts and Letters.'

'Fantastic. Bon voyage.' Frank stood up.

'Good luck on your last day at the Times. Brilliant things are coming. I know it. I'm looking forward to reading something great soon, Frank.'

Frank remembered to air kiss Joanna and felt stupid. He watched her go. Mick Jordan had left his table and a new place had been laid. Frank signed the bill. He looked at the view. The Hudson was churning, miniature people on the street below; workers toiled in their offices like hamsters in cages. The drum beat of business and money. A smell hit his nostrils, almost indescribable – sweat, mint, oil, bananas, tobacco, posh industrial cleaning product, coffee, heat, bergamot, and celery all at once. It was success. That sweet smell. He had smelt it once before, ten years ago. Back then he had nothing to lose. He was hungry. He wanted that feeling again. Frank needed a crime to kickstart his new book.

RICHARD JERRAM

Richard Jerram embarked on a new career as a crime fiction writer after years of using his doctorate from the LSE to work as an economist in London, Tokyo and Singapore. His first novel, *The Makoto Murders,* won the Crime Writers' Association's Debut Dagger award in 2024.

tokyotipster15@gmail.com

The Makoto Murders

The opening of a novel

CHAPTER ONE – MODEL

Click. Click.

She was perfect. Born to be photographed. Sprawled across the floor, without a care in the world. Right leg straight, the other bent towards the window. Arms arranged loosely on each side. Shoulder-length hair scattered in a black halo. White blouse with sleeves ending halfway down her forearms. Black skirt, riding up to give a glimpse of thigh.

Click.

Perfect except for the red ligature mark around her neck, mottled with purple bruises. Fingernail scratches too, as she'd struggled to relieve the pressure on her windpipe. A stream of urine ran alongside her legs and pooled by her feet. And the smell, showing her bowels had evacuated.

I only cared about the visuals.

She was perfect for me. For my ambitions. The scene felt curated to highlight the tragedy of a life ended so abruptly. I took a moment to pinch my nose and started to breathe through my mouth.

Click. Click.

I adjusted the flash to give her a softer tone. High cheekbones. Unblemished skin with a small mole just to the right of her nose. Such a cute, natural nose too, not pointed in a way that might have suggested a weekend trip over the Sea of Japan to the plastic surgeons of Seoul. Neatly groomed eyebrows.

Click.

Just my type. Slim, without being skinny. Well turned out. A seven. Maybe even an eight. Shame. I held the camera above my head, looking for a wider perspective. Something that would capture the ordinary, everyday nature of the scene, in contrast to the extraordinary spectacle of murder. I wanted the background of the kitchenette just in from the door. Pots drying in the rack after a final, solitary dinner. A calendar pinned to the wall by the fridge pointed to an active social life. Tracking down some of the scribbled names would keep the police busy for a while.

A low table sat on the tatami mats in the living room, surrounded by enough cushions for a guest or two. Magazines piled untidily next to a teapot and single blue cup suggested she hadn't been expecting visitors.

Click. Click.

Behind me, the lift mechanism whirred into action. Inner city neighbourhoods like Ichigaya weren't famous for their sense of community, and buildings full of small apartments probably had plenty of turnover, but still ... I didn't want to be mistaken for the murderer. Even I might stop to look if I came home and found a stranger in the doorway of the place next door, photographing a dead body. In fact, I'd look whoever it was. Professional curiosity.

The lift had been on the fourth floor when I arrived, so I had a moment to think while it descended. I'd taken the stairs up to the victim's unlocked third-storey apartment, happy to avoid any security cameras, and I figured the chances were slim that a resident would surprise me by doing the same. Of course, there was still a danger that someone on this floor might need to go out – a late-night run to the convenience store, or something – but that was a chance I had to take. It was late, so most of the foot traffic should be home-to-bed. As far as I'd been able to tell from the street when I'd arrived, all the third-floor lights, except this one, were off.

Maybe a one-in-five chance the lift was coming to this floor. Not good enough. I had some great material, but I wanted more. This was a blockbuster.

My heart was beating faster now. No way was I going inside and shutting the door behind me. If I contaminated the crime scene, the police would go from being pissed off that I was there first to charging me with interference. And if the lift was bringing her a late-night visitor, they might reasonably ask what I was doing there.

I pushed the door shut with the sleeve of my jacket. Then I hurried through the fire exit at the end of the corridor and tiptoed up to the fourth floor.

Breathing hard with the stress, I waited until my hands were steady enough to run through the pictures I'd already taken. They looked alright – no, they looked wonderful – but I still needed some close-ups. I realised I'd been holding back. Standing in the doorway, hiding behind the camera, I could tell myself I was just an observer. The zoom would put me right there beside her. Bring some sense of participation. Of responsibility. But I needed that shot.

I took a few moments to sync the camera to my phone and send the photos to my work email. We'd discussed it in the editorial meeting after the first body was found. Our lawyers were confident the police weren't allowed to seize my camera or force me to delete the pictures. But we weren't confident they'd know that. And less confident they'd restrain themselves, even supposing they knew the legal limits of their authority.

I copied in my private email too. My editor was going to work himself into an orgasmic frenzy when he saw my haul, but everything is political. Everyone was going to want a say on whether, and how much, to publish. If some high-ranking corporate suit spiked it, I'd have to take the pics across the street. Though it was hard to believe, a couple of our competitors had even fewer scruples than *Hikari* and they'd snatch my hand off if I offered them a deal.

There were way too many to publish. An idea came to me in a rush. Once it was all over, I might even be able to take the more sensitive shots – not the brutal ones *Hikari* wanted – and put out a photobook, just like Daido Moriyama. All in black and white. The sort of thing people leave lying around to act as a conversation starter. Maybe even a gallery exhibition – in Ginza, yes that would be ideal – and sell numbered prints as well.

The second murder in a week. A serial killer in Tokyo? And this time, I had the pictures. This was dynamite. Job-saving, prize-winning, money-making dynamite. One way or another, the public was going to see it. Would demand to see it. Deserved to see it.

I steadied myself against the wall and shut my eyes for a few seconds. Don't get ahead of yourself, Daisuke. There's still work to be done. Out of habit, I checked my Nikon's battery – still three-quarters full – and headed back downstairs.

No sign of life came from the corridor as I paused to listen before opening the fire exit door. No tell-tale sounds of people running up and down, screaming, 'Murder, Murder.'

So it was back to the door of number thirty-two, pulled open with my jacket sleeve again, boot against the door to stop it closing. She looked just as peaceful as before. Just as perfect.

This time I started by kneeling in the doorway, putting myself on the same level as her. As equals. Well, except for the fact she was stone-cold dead, and I was still trying to carve out some kind of a life.

She seemed more vulnerable from that angle. Asking us to imagine the way her attacker had done his evil deed – and I was sure it was a 'he' – before letting her crash to the floor. It was hard to imagine her muscles ever had the power, or co-ordination, to hold this frail assortment of bones upright. To follow instructions from the brain, flowing down the spine, to balance well enough to walk to the kitchenette and make tea, or draw the curtains, or open the door to see who was calling so late in the evening.

I'd been travelling light, so I didn't have my usual range of gear. Still, my basic flash had enough power to reinforce the light of the room, and it was plenty for the short distance from the door. I took a few of her upper thighs as well, with a hint of the panties beyond. That would appeal to a pervier sub-set of our readers, but I was doubtful the editor would run them. The victim didn't seem to mind, but there are limits.

We often lack the sense to know how much is enough. I know I do. Keep doing the same thing even though the marginal benefits have shrunk to zero. Or even negative, in the case of whisky. So I stayed there too long, not adding anything worthwhile to the bank of pictures I'd already taken. Maybe I didn't want to leave her alone on that cold, friendless floor.

Not that she gave any sign of thanks, but I promised I'd find someone to take care of her. To ensure a smooth passage out of this world and into the next, if it existed. So she could avoid the ignominy of being eaten by cats – not that she had any – or her neighbour calling the building administrators in a couple of weeks, to complain about the terrible smell coming from apartment thirty-two.

The lift took me downstairs.

Once I was outside, I dialled 110.

CHAPTER TWO – ON THE SCENE

Society frowns on some forms of double-dipping. Like putting your half-eaten *kushiage* stick back into the communal pot of sauce for another coating. But I was definitely going to be double-dipping on the murder, with action photographs of the cops arriving to complement those of the main event inside apartment thirty-two. After all, I'd been the one to find her. No chance I was going to miss out on an extension of my exclusive, so I popped a can of hot coffee out of a vending machine and leant against a nearby wall to wait.

As I stood there enjoying my drink, I could already glimpse another award ceremony on the horizon. Name in lights, winning photo on display, jealous competitors seething at their tables around the room. My boss choking as he swallowed the redundancy notice he'd been preparing. The last ceremony had been good. Fantastic, even. Winning twice would show it wasn't a fluke.

When I'd won before, back in 2011, there'd been plenty of competition. Earthquake, tsunami, nuclear meltdown – the biggest catastrophe since the war, so it produced lots of good copy. This year was disappointingly peaceful. No major disasters, nothing very sensational. Murders of single men and women were going to be right up there, especially with my exclusive, up-close snaps.

Power. I could already feel it. The rush of winning. The invincibility.

I threw my arms out, like DiCaprio in *Titanic*. King of the World. Dregs of coffee slopped out onto the back of my hand, bringing me back to the present. I licked them off. This could be enough to bring Makoto back to me. I knew she liked a winner, and I could already see her modelling the dresses she would be thinking about wearing for the gala dinners.

To be fair, it didn't take the cops long to show up. Then again, the sniff of a murder is a big thing, even in a city the size of Tokyo. Not like America, where they stab, strangle, shoot or otherwise slay their fellow citizens about as often as we have traffic accidents on this side of the Pacific.

They must have time-wasters calling in day and night. Especially when it's late and drunks or losers are trying to entertain their sad souls by pranking the cops. So they only sent a single patrol car. Still, I scored a few good shots as it pulled up. Lights flashing, but no siren. Two uniforms jumped out and the one from the passenger seat – senior one, I imagined; he looked older, more out of shape – consulted a notebook before heading in the wrong direction.

'It's over here,' I called across and made sure I had my Nikon ready for when they turned and came towards me.

They waved the camera away as they approached.

'You the one that called it in?'

Not the brightest, most cops. How many other people did they see standing around outside a murder victim's apartment block at one-thirty in the morning? Apart from a few cars, nobody had come past since I'd dialled those three digits.

For an answer, I thrust my press pass at them.

It's not the sort of thing cops like. They want to be able to get on with their job, however incompetently or dishonestly, without the prying eyes of the fourth estate. But I wasn't going to risk having them drag me up to apartment thirty-two and smear my fingerprints around her place. Add to their implausibly high conviction rate.

I swear I saw the younger one's lips moving when he was reading my particulars. The older, fatter one was more focused on wiping his sleeve across his forehead. It was a cool October evening and he'd barely walked twenty paces from the car, so I guessed the excitement was all too much for him.

My credentials seemed to be enough to convince them of the truth behind my emergency call, and they bustled past me and into the building's lobby to investigate. The guns, handcuffs and nightsticks flapping on their belts weren't going to see any action that night, unless they decided I was too much of a smartarse.

I followed, more for entertainment value than the chance of a decent picture.

They stood in front of the closed door to the building. The junior guy – the driver – gave it a pull, only confirming they needed a key to make it open.

The senior one seemed to feel the need to show his authority, so he gave it a pull as well. Then he used his initiative, though not his brains, and pressed the keypad to dial apartment thirty-two. It rang out, but no one answered.

I was pleased about that. If she'd done a Lazarus on me, then I could flush those photos.

They looked at each other and consulted their notes again. I was hoping one would take off his cap and scratch his head, but they weren't that animated. The driver sucked his teeth instead, but that's not visual enough for me.

I figured it was time to lend a hand. We'd be there all night.

'The lock on the side gate has been busted open. You can get in that way.'

'Stay right there,' the senior one cautioned, though I'd already have been long gone if I'd wanted. Without any further clues, they managed to find the door that led to the waste bins and bicycle storage area, and from there, into the building itself. Not that your standard killer is much smarter than the cops – or they wouldn't keep getting caught – but this one must have realised that most residential buildings only have a security camera in the main entrance lobby.

When I'd arrived an hour earlier, I'd gone in the back way too, after checking the front door was locked. They'd find me on tape from the security camera, once I was finished upstairs, after I walked out the lift and into the lobby before pulling open the mailbox for apartment thirty-two. Checked a couple of letters to make sure I had her name right. Makoto Tanaka.

Two Makotos in a row. Of course, the first one had been male. I wondered if the police would see it as a pattern or a coincidence. It's a fairly common name, more for men than women, though out of fashion in recent years. Probably not too many under the age of twenty. The victim upstairs looked in her early thirties.

I knew what they were going to find, so I went back outside to wait, and this time the turnout was more impressive. Three patrol cars and one unmarked sedan, with an ambulance not far behind. Flashers and sirens. Uniforms and plain clothes. I couldn't see the need for them to hurry, but at least it was more photogenic than the initial turnout, so I snapped away happily. I took some good shots of the gurney as they wheeled it in, which would make a nice contrast when it came out burdened by her body.

It was all too late for Makoto Tanaka, but at least it showed they cared. She might have died a lonely and terrified death in some corner of Ichigaya, but at least she hadn't been abandoned.

And I was going to make her famous.

CHAPTER THREE – INSPECTOR SASAKI

It was still early morning when they took Makoto Tanaka away. I shot some decent pictures of the indecent scene, but by that time, the competition had got wind of the action and they'd rocked up on motorbikes or in taxis. That meant nothing else was exclusive, so it wasn't as much value as what I already had, but it would round out the narrative. At least the media pack would ensure top billing for the story on the news and make my haul even more precious.

We always have an eye out for whoever is first on the scene and word must've got around that it was me. Omura from *Kagami* must have recognised my Yamaha and was having a smoke where I'd parked. He flicked the butt into the gutter when I came over and unclipped my helmet.

'Hey, Kato-kun. Bit early in the day for you, isn't it?'

Omura wasn't a bad guy. He'd been one of the few whose congratulations had felt genuine after I'd won the Big One. In fact, I was surprised he hadn't won it himself yet – his work was that good. He didn't just put it on automatic and click away, volume over value, then sift through the output looking for gems. His trademark was to use the override to set a small f-stop, so the wide aperture blurred the background and drew all the focus on to the subject. It was high risk and didn't always work, but when it did, the effect was really powerful.

'You know what they say, *hayaoki wa sanmon no toku*.'

'I always had you for more of a night owl,' he replied. 'How d'you get here so fast?'

I made a show of looking around to make sure we weren't being overheard. 'Truth is Omura-kun, I haven't even been home yet. Just happened to be in the neighbourhood seeing a friend, really late, if you know what I mean. So I ducked down here.'

He gave me an admiring nod and expressed an appropriate level of jealousy. Then, after some inconsequential chat, he left me to it. Of course, he'd realise what I'd told him wasn't true as soon as he saw the shots of Makoto Tanaka in *Hikari*, but I'd be gone by then. We could share a joke or a coffee, but no one was under any illusions about the need to be honest with each other. Not if it might get in the way of a good story.

The reminder of how late it was – or early, depending on your perspective – made me realise I was exhausted. Hungry too. I'd been so absorbed in the murder and the scoop that the adrenalin had overridden any physical needs, and now they were catching up in a rush. It wasn't quite five and the sky was just beginning to lighten in the east. I decided there was time to shoot home for a quick nap and a shower before heading into the office to look at my haul more closely and figure out how we were going to handle things. I could have gone in straight away, but from now on, things were going to run on our lawyers' schedule, and I wanted to be fresh to deal with them.

I'd swung my leg over the seat and was putting the key into the ignition when a tallish guy in a dark jacket hurried across. He called out my name and waved his badge at me at the same time, so I couldn't pretend I hadn't seen him and dash off into the dawn. I was still tempted, but he moved so quickly, I would've had to run him down to get away.

'I'm Sasaki. Inspector in the Tokyo Metropolitan Police.'

He traded his badge for a notebook while I pulled off my helmet and gripped it tight in my left hand. This was going to be more serious than the two clowns I'd met earlier. I introduced myself and gave my affiliation, but he still took the time to take a close look at my press pass, making a few notes in his book.

'You're the one that called it in.'

I wasn't sure if it was a question, but if it was, we both knew the answer. The uniforms had already taken my contact details – the junior one sticking his tongue half out in concentration as he copied down my name. Sasaki looked more capable, and I figured there was no upside in teasing him, so I nodded and grunted a confirmation.

The streetlight must have caught me in a certain way and made him stop and look at me more closely. I knew what was coming next.

'Are you *hāfu*?'

'What's your point, Inspector?'

'You're *hāfu*, right?'

'I'm Japanese,' I answered. I wasn't going to play that game, not at that time in the morning. In fact, not at any time, unless I was flirting with a girl in a bar, and she thought it was cool. Some mixed-race people I knew described themselves as 'double' rather than 'half' or '*hāfu*,' with its racist undertones, but that always sounded annoyingly smug to me.

Sasaki didn't seem to know what to do with my answer, so he returned to the task at hand.

'What were you doing here?'

This was where it could get sticky. The lawyers had been over it in detail, role-playing the approaches the police might take. Normally, I'm not a great one for meetings, but this time, I'd given the suits my full attention. Listen and repeat, as those tapes used to say when we were learning French in school.

'I'm a journalist for *Hikari* magazine.' I held up my press pass to illustrate the claim, even though he'd just seen it. '*Hikari* magazine received a tip about a crime at this location. I came to investigate the story.'

Sasaki frowned. 'I get that. But how did you know to come here?'

By now, I was getting a bit distracted, as his voice was a lot deeper than it had any right to be, based on his medium build. I wanted to stuff my lens down his throat to see if there was a bigger, fatter man hiding in there. But the stakes were high, so I concentrated at staying on message.

'I'm a journalist for *Hikari* magazine. *Hikari* magazine received a tip about a crime at this location. I came to investigate the story.' I didn't bother to hold out my pass the second time around.

Sasaki ran through a few more permutations of his basic question in his solid baritone, his frown turning to a scowl as I graced him with a consistent answer. I imagine he might have wanted to drag me down an alley to express his displeasure in a more physical way, but he was probably deterred by the watching press corps. Some of them would have cheered him on, but that wouldn't have stopped them from taking a few pictures.

He paused for a minute and fixed me with a stare, as if he was wondering what to do next. I guessed it was his best 'suspect intimidation' look that he practised in front of the mirror. Maybe they even had contests at HQ.

'Inspector, do you have a minute?' A uniformed officer called across to Sasaki, while holding a phone above his head and rocking it back and forth.

I put my helmet back on to show I had places I needed to be. Flipped the visor open. They're usually reluctant to tangle with the press, but there was a risk he might carry me off to the station to see if I could be persuaded to be any more co-operative after I'd been locked in a small room for a few hours. Fatigue was eating away at me, and I was desperate to go home.

'Inspector, I can see you're busy,' I said. 'Look, I want to help, but our lawyers told me... well, you know what they're like.' I shrugged. Only following orders. 'I've seen the same things you have in number thirty-two. Take my business card and we can talk later. I'll be in the office.'

That seemed to do the trick. After we'd exchanged *meishi* so he had my contact details, I was allowed to go on my way. Inspector Tsuyoshi Sasaki, it said on his. I took another look to burn him into my memory bank. Recent haircut, but still over his collar. Piercing eyes that gave no hint of cynicism or disillusionment, even at this ungodly hour. Skin that said he'd never been a smoker. Good quality suit; understated not flash. The case was going to be almost as big for him as it was for me, so I knew I was going to be seeing plenty more of Inspector Sasaki.

Despite my exhaustion, or maybe because of it, I felt a sense of tranquillity on the ride home to Shinagawa. There was almost no traffic, so it wasn't the usual life-or-death experience of riding an underpowered motorbike through Tokyo. I even decided to take the most direct route, via Roppongi crossing, which would be jammed solid at any reasonable hour. There might be a few dazed stragglers heading home, but not the usual crush of taxis vying for business.

No, it was more than tranquillity. More like a sense that things were going my way again after a few tough years. There was still plenty of work to be done, but I had some great pictures, and I was sure my editor would be on board. My guess on how the photos would play with the readers was somewhere on the scale between fantastic and sensational.

This was what made photojournalism – press photography – such good fun. I'd done some for my school newspaper in England and in the university club at Waseda, which had been enough to land me the position at *Hikari*. One of the best things about it is you can't do the work sitting around the office. Of course, there are plenty of dull bits, like any job. Such as doorstepping some idiot who's hiding away at home after being caught putting his dick where he shouldn't. But there's lots of time when you're out chasing a story, trying to get there ahead of the pack. Aiming for the shot that's going to take that week's cover. The pictures on the memory card in my Nikon were going to dominate the whole magazine, not just the cover.

This story was mine. And I had a plan to make it run for weeks, unlike the one-off shot that won me the Prize four years ago. I wondered how long I needed to wait until I started rehearsing another victory speech.

VALERIE MCGUIRE

Valerie McGuire is an archival detective and a cultural historian of the Mediterranean based in Austin TX. She has a PhD in Italian Studies from New York University and is a published academic author. Oil and Wine, her first novel, incorporates her passion for geographies at the margins of history.

vmcguire@utexas.edu
www.valerie-mcguire.com

Oil and Wine

The opening of a novel

CHAPTER ONE – AT THE GRAVE OF PERCY SHELLEY

I had finished writing my story and was packing up to leave when I sensed from behind a short and stalky presence dashing toward me. It was Mario, my ex. His dress shirt was matted to his chest like a sheet after an afternoon of heavy lovemaking.

'Oh, Flaminia, I found you. Thank goodness,' he said, breathless. An inveterate smoker first and one of the most determined people you could ever meet as a close second, Mario raced toward any objective he sought, regardless of smog or natural disaster, and then lit up when he got there. 'I figured you were here.'

'The Pope's interview with the President of Jordan in Castel Gandolfo.'

'Exactly. Did you get what you need?'

'I think so.' The President of Jordan had given the Pope a figure to keep the refugees in her country. In a couple of days, she would go to Brussels and collect the money. 'A pro forma meeting.'

'Sounds about right,' said Mario. His pug nose twitched like a little rabbit with peremptory understanding. He nodded quickly and gestured toward the thick frosted glass doors of the press hall, beyond which appeared a wedge of bold and unforgiving sunlight. He needed a smoke. 'Let's walk and get a coffee,' he added more gently. 'I'll explain.'

Heat had ripped through Rome like a tide flushing out a harbor all summer long. The temperature had shot to boiling and the pressure ticked up. A muggy cloud had settled over the city; the motorcycle fumes and scent of trash could not escape, only the wealthy. Every day, I had come downtown to the foreigners' press hall—to use the free air conditioning. Along with the heat, all summer long refugees had poured into Europe. The Caritas centers in Italy were full and there were more coming.

We were like dough fired into an oven outside, the cobblestones hot little bricks under our feet. We coasted along the side of buildings taking shade from the rafters like sailboats leveraging the breeze off an island until we reached a large piazza converted into a parking lot. A sirocco wind had sanded the cars overnight and it looked like a dune. Mario pointed to a small and nameless bar, one without tables or chairs, no more than a dark little cavern, where no doubt the coffee would be thick and delicious and as strong as gasoline.

We were the only customers, and Mario spoke in barely a whisper. 'This morning the police found a dead body — above ground — in the non-Catholic cemetery.' He swirled the espresso in his cup, letting the information sink in. 'The body was laid, just like an offering, at the grave of Percy Shelley.' He downed the coffee in one gulp and gestured for another one. The owner, a frail and elderly gentleman, blended in with the antique bar of marble and oak.

'Why are you telling me?' I wondered aloud.

'It's not the kind of story I get to write anymore,' said Mario ruefully. I tried to gauge his sincerity. Mario lived and died by his job at the National Press Service, but he liked to bleat on about being chained to a desk. His flushed face showed no signs of subterfuge.

'Thanks,' I said flatly. 'And so, you thought you would offer it to me.'

Mario disregarded my comment. 'Great story potential,' he went on. 'I say we go and see what we can find out. You can write up a brief. And then, if the boss likes it, maybe you can write a longer story when more information becomes available.'

'I have other plans this afternoon.' My plans were vague, but I didn't like where we were heading — which was back toward a short-term contract at the press service.

Never one to balk in the face of resistance, Mario soldiered on. 'In a few hours, the police will have cleared the scene. There's nothing like going to the actual scene, you know that.' He contorted his face into a grimace that said he had known I would be difficult. 'Your plans, whatever they are, they can be postponed. This can't.'

The bar owner looked over at me and gave me a kind and almost angelic smile. 'Well, let's go then,' I said, surprising even myself.

Later I asked why I caved to Mario so readily. I chalked it up to the heat, humidity, and those fine grains of dust sprayed everywhere, blanking out my mind like the sandstorm that had come from the Sahara across the sea to Rome.

The police had blocked off the street that led to the main entrance by the Pyramid of Cestius and we took a long detour on Mario's motorcycle and approached the cemetery from the other direction. Here we met another blockade. We were allowed to pass after showing our press credentials. On the other side of the main gate cypress trees stood guard like sentinels on a slope cramped with gravestones. Mario remembered that the cemetery was roughly organized from oldest to most recent arrivals.

We were heading off toward the ancient quadrant of the park when an attractive, well-dressed, and dainty but sour-faced young woman holding a short-wave radio intercepted us. 'You can find the team at the tomb of Gramsci,' she said. With her free arm, she made an exaggerated jag, like a member of a Martha Graham modernist dance troupe, and pointed down a narrow footpath leading through the park.

'The police certainly have a sense of irony,' muttered Mario under his breath as he heel-pivoted in the direction that the policewoman had zagged us. 'As if we need a reminder that international Marxism is dead.'

Mario had long since destroyed his membership card to the Italian communist party, but he clung to the idea that the police were crypto fascists in homage to his former, more anarchic self.

We reversed course and headed toward the twentieth century where space was tight. Each grave marker barely fitted within a plot, family members added to existing tombs, whole communities placed beneath ground. We reached a large monument with a park bench: the tomb of Gramsci. A policeman was busy collecting data on tablets while another man siloed himself from the rest seeming to preside over the park's stony silence. It had to be the inspector.

'Benedetti,' the man said when we were close enough. For a moment, Benedetti looked us over emptily. He seemed to lumber to speech. 'The lead on the investigation this morning. You arrived just in time. In about thirty minutes the body will be transported to Benefratelli hospital.'

'De Luca. From ANSA. We came as soon as we heard. You will know better, but it's not often that there's a homicide in the historic center.'

'We haven't ruled out suicide,' replied Benedetti. 'But you're right—we don't often find a dead body on this side of the GRA.' *The Grande Raccordo Anulare*, the giant ring road that rivered around Rome like a moat annulling poverty from the historic center.

'We heard you found the body lying at the grave of Percy Shelly. Is that true?'

Benedetti nodded slowly but offered no more. His blue dress shirt clung to his chest like a wet blanket. He still managed to look elegant.

Mario looked over with urgent eyes, telling me it was my turn to ask a question.

'Flaminia Bonifazi. I cover the crime beat for *Il Messaggero* and *Il Mattino*,' I lied. I hadn't written a crime story in three years, not since my son was born. My beat was culture now, and I wanted to keep it that way. But I obliged my ex. Old habits die hard. 'Can we see the scene?' A crowing bird drowned out the crackle in my voice.

Benedetti gestured for us to follow him. The National Press Service opened every door. He led us across the crest of the cemetery along a narrow trail that hugged the ancient city walls. The ground was uneven and in places grave markers leaned like sunken towers; in some places, the tombstones seemed to reach toward one another. The sight begged the question if it was as cramped below and if it ever happened that, when they dug to inter a new arrival, they ran into the remains of someone else.

Benedetti pointed to a small clearing where we should stand, on the other side of a makeshift barrier of tape and traffic cones. Nearby a circle had worn away in the ancient walls. Bright sunlight poured like an unwanted floodlight illuminating a white sheet over a lifeless body. Not far away was Shelley's headstone with the famous epitaph from Shakespeare's *Tempest*: 'Nothing of him that doth fade but doth suffer a sea-change into something rich and strange.'

Benedetti crouched down at one end. 'No photos,' he said, and drew the sheet back quickly, like a chambermaid stripping a bed.

The man was not much darker than the sheet that had been covering him. His face was already a sallow lifeless color, crowned by a thick rush of coal-black hair. His mouth and eyes were both open, giving the impression of horrible fright. At his right temple, where the hair was matted with blood, a determined fly buzzed.

Benedetti spoke. 'As you can see, the location of the headwound fairly rules out a suicide though that is of course unofficial until we release the coroner's report.'

'Is there any chance that the body was brought here?' asked Mario. The shade of the large umbrella pines cooled the cemetery. When the sun moved out from behind one of the trees, we were bathed in the heat again. Mario strained his eyes in the face of the purple light. 'If it was homicide — and it seems that's the hypothesis you're working with — what are the chances that it could have happened somewhere else in the cemetery, even closer to the entrance?' He shaded his forehead with a hand. 'Is it possible that he could have been fatally wounded someplace else and then dragged himself over to this grave, say, to leave some kind of message?'

Benedetti pushed sweat away from his brow. He seemed interested but then his expression evaporated into annoyance. 'We're not here to read the crime scene like a detective novel. Apart from the difficulties of dragging a dead body — or dragging oneself — the prints suggest death happened here,' said Benedetti. He walked a half-circle around the body seeking the shade of one of the umbrella pines.

'Signs of struggle?' insisted Mario.

Benedetti sighed. 'Yes, we identified a few contusions. The coroner's report will tell us more.'

At the mention of bruises, I saw that the sheet had only been peeled as far as the dead man's shoulders. 'Could we see the whole body?' I asked.

Benedetti nodded and drew the rest of the sheet back.

The man wore a pair of loose-fitting checked trousers and a starched white smock: a cook's uniform. At the bottom of his body, two small naked feet peered out like small little morning birds. 'We already bagged the shoes for evidence,' said the inspector, seeing my confusion. He replaced the sheet over the body.

Benedetti led us back across the spine of the cemetery. The team had cleared the tomb of Gramsci, save the scarecrow woman who had stopped us at the gate. Instead of a short-wave radio, she held a clipboard now. 'Another call has come in, *dottore*,' she said to Benedetti. 'You're wanted in *Questura*.'

Passing his card to Mario and giving a half-apologetic smile, the inspector bade an end to our interview. 'Duty calls. If you have any other questions, you can call later this afternoon.'

'Oh, one last question,' said Mario, as if it were an afterthought. 'Do you have an ID yet on the body?'

'We do. But we can't disclose that information until after the coroner's report.'

Back at his motorcycle, Mario passed me his extra passenger's helmet. 'Let's go discuss. I know a place.' Only Mario could think about food after the sight of a man dead in cold blood.

We weaved through the back alleys of Testaccio, the old meat-packing district, until Mario led us to a brightly lit coffee shop called Safi's Place. Inside a capacious hall that looked to have been adapted from a former horse stable were large, corrugated metal tables splashed with shadows made by designer lighting. Around the tables were benches covered in brightly colored cushions made from Indian saris. It was the sort of place that ten years would have been thought unimaginable. A place for smart-working where people brought their laptops and yammered in video meetings for hours.

'I've been hired to write a short review of vegan restaurants,' Mario explained.

'Naturally,' I replied. Mario rarely ate a meal without billing it to someone else.

'The tourists come here in the afternoon for a *capraccino*.'

'A *capraccino?*'

'A cappuccino made of goat milk!' Unable to contain himself, Mario let out a huge chortle from his belly that caused him to wheeze.

'I thought you said it was a vegan place.'

'Vegan, gluten free, no GMO, biological, Slow Food, No Global, this place is a mishmash of whatever is du jour. No one cares.'

I ordered a green tea and began fingering the mirrored eyelets of the magenta-colored sari cushion below me.

'Perhaps the victim's murderer was a lover, and it was a crime of passion,' said Mario after ordering a vegan pizza. 'Or maybe they didn't know each other, and it was a hot date gone wrong, so to speak.'

I looked at him blankly.

'"The Ashes of Gramsci"?'

'The Ashes of Gramsci' was a famous poem by the iconoclast Pier Paolo Pasolini—hero of the Left, champion of the Roman periphery — in which an international Marxist revolution is reignited by an act of casual sex in the non-Catholic cemetery, right next to the very tomb of Gramsci where we had just been. 'Mario, I don't think anyone has been cruising in that cemetery since the 1970s.'

'Why else would the police set up at the tomb of Gramsci?'

'Got you,' I said with mock bravado. I couldn't tell if Mario was being serious, or just warming to a point.

'They already have an ID on the victim,' he continued, 'That can mean only one of two things.'

I recalled the man's bare feet. To have identified the victim meant that there were fingerprints — more likely, footprints — on record in a database. A criminal. But now immigrants were required by law to submit their biometric information, in exchange for which they sometimes got residency papers. 'That the victim was either a criminal or an immigrant.'

'The cook's uniform says immigrant.'

'Or not,' I replied. I thought of the man's sallow face and coal-black hair. He could have just as easily been from one of our villages in the South, where we were all of Arab extraction anyway. 'How many from our region work in restaurants in this city?'

Mario chafed and gulped water to swallow his irritation. We had been that proverbial hometown couple. As the saying goes, *meglio mogli e buoi dal paese tuo*: better to get bulls and wives from your own village. We had lasted almost a year together after we both moved to Rome. Mario had wanted to get married and *fare figli*. But we were too close and too alike to survive. Our differences had been like lesions, always there and just under the surface and ready to boil up to become a battle over our profoundly different life philosophies. Money had been a sore point.

'I don't know what else you have going on right now, but I am willing to bet it won't pay as much as this story.'

I thought of the Sufi group that I had been planning to contact before Mario had found me at the press hall. I said nothing knowing exactly what kind of reaction I would get. 'And why are you trying to help me?' I replied tersely.

'Because I am your friend.'

'Friend,' I echoed taking a sip of my green tea. I was not at all sure I agreed.

'Yes, friend,' he said. He sounded convinced.

Mario gave a long sigh of frustration when I said nothing. He was done trying to knock sense into me about a good story when it was handed to me. He paid for the green tea and vegan pizza that he declared an absolute offense to humanity, and we hurriedly abandoned the vegan restaurant called Safi's Place.

I asked Mario to drop me off at the river. It was too late now to work on another story, and I felt out of sorts. A walk would clear my head, despite the heat. Since having a child my days were so packed that I no longer had time to wander, something every good writer needs. For a moment I stood there dumbly looking around. I realized with a jolt that the daylight was beginning to dim, and that homeward-bound traffic had already begun. Soon I too would have to rush home. On an impulse, I plunged down the stairs to the banks of the river.

Not everyone was in a hurry to go home. When I was level with the river, I caught sight of a gangly man passing a long stick with thatch over the ground. I thought it was a city worker until when I got close enough and saw that the man did not wear a uniform but a long and gauzy tunic. I recognized him to be one of the Bangladeshi trinket sellers who sometimes set up a blanket outside the press hall. With his makeshift broom, he was sweeping up the trash. Nestled at the foot of the tall brick retaining walls of the river were two piles, one with the trash and then another smaller one with various bric-à-brac: a metal cigarette lighter, a cell phone charger, a selfie stick, a large and floral printed pencil case that likely had contained a young woman's toiletries. He planned to clean and try to resell it all. One had to wonder how such objects became so thoughtlessly unmoored from their owners. And be thankful that there was someone out there who could see their potential as treasure.

The man seemed to recognize me. As I passed, he rested the broom on the walls and stretched out his stringy arms like an eagle about to take flight. For a moment I feared he would lurch and wrap his arms around me. Instead, he yelled out, 'God has given me two arms!' Then he gave a crooked smile that revealed two decayed teeth and the blunted pain of a life of misery.

I did my best to smile back and match his exuberance. After a few seconds it occurred to me to yell out, 'And two legs!'

The trinket seller nodded solemnly and nearly bowed. Then he picked up his broom and went back to sweeping. I looked away, toward the river's green waters rushing by, not wanting to make eye contact a second time.

I hurried on and at the next set of stairs hiked back up to street level.

I was headed back to the press hall to collect my scooter when I remembered it was my night for dinner. I swung quickly to the right and into one of the narrow streets that led to the Jewish ghetto where there was a small trattoria that had a take-out window.

The area still had tourists sitting outside eating fried artichokes, but they were fewer now that it was almost the end of August. Soon the tables would be pulled up and the pedestrian way that cut straight through the Jewish ghetto and led to the synagogue — now barricaded and patrolled by armed guards like the American embassy — would be empty and the view of the theater of Marcellus uninterrupted by table parasols.

At the entrance of the trattoria, I stopped in my tracks as an image of the dead man thumped to the front of my head like a migraine. It had been three years since I left the crime beat and I had gone soft in the meantime. It made me queasy, having to hold the image of the man's wide-open stare on his grey face; his matted black hair, where the bullet had entered and pierced all life out of him; the dried-up, crusting blood. I hadn't eaten since breakfast but felt I might have to run to a nearby alley and wretch up those hungry gastric juices. The first rule of working on a crime story was not to take an interest in the victim but only in the authorities investigating it. But I had left the crime beat because I didn't believe in rules, or at least not ones I hadn't made myself. And now I was wondering if the victim was like me and had a family, and what he would have been doing right then — had he still been alive — to feed it.

I reached the front of the queue and ordered some oily eggplant parmesan that Melik would hate but be too polite to say. For Alain, my son, I bought large and flat roasted potatoes that were like mushy french fries, which he would love. Then I asked for some double pan-fried chicory so we would eat something green. A working woman's idea of a healthy family meal.

'Is everything all right, signora?'

I looked up and saw the shop owner staring kindly at me. He was waiting for me to take my white plastic bags of food away so he could serve the next person in line.

'Of course,' I said smiling lightly. 'Thank you for asking.'

I grabbed the food and hustled out of the trattoria. Now the early evening homebound traffic rushed by me. I felt bloated and lethargic, and I stumbled off to the side to stand out of the way. Around my collar and my back, I was damp with sweat. But I still felt cold.

I passed a small park where mothers with prams and toddlers were gathering for some fresh air after the long afternoon at home. I looked at the women, trying to guess how many of them were nannies or babysitters. Some of them looked like young mothers today. It made me think of who I might have become had I married Mario when we were younger, and he had asked.

I sat down next to one of the mothers on a park bench. I gave a little friendly smile, careful not to look like I wanted to start chatting. I knew well how lonely it could be to watch a child all day. I opened my phone and began looking for the famous sonnet. I dwelled on the last few lines: 'Nothing beside remains round the decay, of that colossal wreck, boundless and bare. The lone and level sands stretch far away.' I thought of the dead man in the cemetery, the beaten-down trinket seller collecting trash at the river and then Mario's dogged ambition and relentless thirst to scoop his colleagues.

I sent my ex a text. 'Thanks for the jaunt down memory lane, just like old times, and the fascinating lead.' A colossal wreck, I started to write. But then I thought better of it. 'Find someone else to pursue it — it's not for me.'

BRIAN MEECHAN

Brian Meechan runs his own communications company and has produced arts programmes including for Radio 4. He's been a BBC correspondent and presenter covering business and politics. Brian's a co-founder, co-director and chair of the Cardiff Book Festival. He's received a writing bursary from Literature Wales. He's originally from Glasgow.

brianmeechan@staygoldmedia.co.uk
X – @brianmeechan
www.linkedin.com/in/brianmeechan

While We Slept

The opening of a novel

CHAPTER ONE
May 2010

Aretha Franklin's searing demand for respect reached its climax. Gemma's fingers danced over the keys of the laptop as she typed. Leaning back on the beige sofa, her head bobbed to the beat, the headphones a welcome barrier to the world around her.

Gemma flinched from the light slap to her right shin. 'Oi,' she yelped, removing the headphones.

'Get your feet off the table,' her mum said as she pulled her hand back. Gemma lowered her feet to the floor. Her white socks with their blackened soles rested on the wooden floorboards. 'Such a filthy habit. I don't know where you get it from.'

'Never a need for violence,' Gemma mumbled.

'Violence,' Sue tutted.

Gemma blew her ginger fringe out of her eyes. She badly needed a haircut, but not as badly as she needed to save money. The stray strands were a constant irritant, but she thought she could live with it for another week. Maybe two.

Sue stacked three small white plates on top of each other and lifted them from the table along with Gemma's coffee mug. Gemma glanced around her at the TV, thinking it would be rude to just put her headphones back on but hoping for some sort of distraction.

'Don't you worry, I'll get your plates,' Sue said.

'Just leave them. I'll do it in a minute.'

'It's fine. I'll get them out the way,' Sue said.

Fuckin' martyr.

In the corner of the living room, a blizzard of statistics streamed from the television. Conservatives gained somewhere posh sounding… Wirral-on-the-Wye or some such… with a twenty-one-thousand-something majority. Lib Dems took a seat with three hundred votes or so. Labour down six-point-whatever per cent on last time. Somebody said the Tories needed ten more seats to form a government. It had been like this all day. Chaos unscrolling. Details without meaning.

'You should be watching this,' her mum said as the TV captured her attention. 'You're supposed to be a journalist.'

'Not that kind of journalist,' Gemma said. Her mother grunted. Not any kind of journalist was Gemma's translation. Two women, one permanent state of mutual exhaustion with each other.

'This is important. It's about the future. For God's sake, you're thirty years old. You need to...' The exact nature of the need seemed to elude Sue.

'They're all the same,' Gemma said. She swatted her hand as though dismissing a troublesome fly and returned her attention to her laptop screen.

'Oh, you don't remember this lot in charge, m'lady. You're about to find out they're nothing like all the same. You'll find out the hard way.'

Gemma could sense her mother still standing there and glanced up. She saw Sue frozen on the spot, transfixed by the TV. Gemma stared at her. A parade of platitudes poured from the screen. Gemma glanced back at it to see what fascinating information she was missing.

Sue noticed her daughter's attention and shook her head slightly. Back from another world. She shuffled towards the kitchen.

'Did you even vote?' her mother stopped to ask, but Gemma had gone back to typing on her laptop. 'No, that's the problem with your lot. Apathy. Your apathy will be the death of us.'

And there it was. A song heard so often that Gemma couldn't distinguish the words but could never mistake the melody. A perennial malcontent that underpinned every interaction. She stopped typing and reached for the black headphones that hung around her neck. Tune out. Rude or not.

Gemma jumped as the plates crashed to the floor. She glared up at her mother in shock. Sue was staring at the TV screen. The dregs of the coffee were splattered across the floor and wall like blood at the scene of a violent crime. The mug lay sideways, its handle broken off.

'What the...' Gemma eyes moved back and forth from her mother to the TV screen. 'What... Mum, what is it?'

Gemma rushed to Sue who appeared torn between the TV and the mess that had been created by the broken crockery. The coffee on the floor soaked into her socks as she took her mum's arm and tried to edge her to the sofa.

'But you're the only Tory MP elected in Scotland, Mr. Hamilton. That's hardly a ringing endorsement of Cameron's compassionate Conservativism, is it?' the TV presenter said, her tone of quiet authority the mark of someone who'd seen all this before.

'Look,' the MP snapped, 'look, this... typical media. Snatching defeat from the jaws of victory as they say. Look, David Cameron is... will be... will *definitely* be the next prime minister. I know the BBC doesn't like that.' He smiled, breathed and sat back in his chair. 'The people have spoken.'

Gemma guided Sue to a seat on the sofa. The older women's attention never wavered from the TV, searching the screen as though the picture was a deceit.

'Platitudes aside, Mr. Hamilton.' The TV presenter smirked, her prey floundering. 'The Conservatives may, or may not, form the next government. We'll see in the coming days. If they do, are you expecting to be the next secretary of state for Scotland?'

Sue sucked in the air around her. Some escaped and she gasped for more. She bent forward.

Gemma held her tighter as her mother began to shake. She followed her eyes to the screen.

'Let's be honest, Mr. Hamilton. You weren't expected to win in that seat. And you're very much on the right of the party. But I suppose David Cameron may not have much choice?' the TV presenter said. Gemma glared at the politician, who squirmed, his face reddening.

'That's... no a question.' His smile had almost been replaced by a snarl before his media training kicked in. 'I'll...' the smile clicked on again, 'I'll serve my country and my constituency in any manner I can.' He nodded, satisfied.

'Bastard,' Sue said.

Gemma flinched at a word she'd never heard from her mother before. The TV screen cut to pictures of David Cameron surrounded by a small, adoring crowd of flag-waving fans.

'Mum, who was that? What's wrong?'

The new images on screen snapped Sue out of it. She seemed confused. Gemma went out of the living room and came back with a glass of water.

'Here. Sip this. I've put the kettle on,' Gemma said as she pushed the glass towards Sue.

Sue busied herself with the mess of broken crockery as though only vaguely aware of how it came to be there. Gemma's questions stalked her mum, but she gave no impression of hearing them.

'Did you have a bit of a funny turn there? Are you not feeling well? It wasn't that man on the telly, was it?'

'Och, I'm fine. Just a wee turn. Don't worry about me.' Sue left the room, carrying the debris. Gemma peered at the TV screen, but it was now redundant as a source.

Above it, a stubborn stain in the top corner of the ceiling looked down on proceedings as it had done for years. No builder could explain or resolve the black damp patch. One cosmetic touch up after another had failed to remove it permanently. Just an old house, they'd inevitably shrug before scurrying away, bored of trying.

Gemma went to her laptop. She flicked on to the Chrome page showing the two-bedroom flat she'd been pining over. Its cosy kitchen with two stools tucked under the breakfast bar. The spacious living room with its three-seater black leather sofa that seemed like you'd never want to leave it. No ugly stain on its ceiling. It even had a balcony, or what her mother would insist on calling a veranda. She closed down the window on the home she could never afford on her small, precarious income. Why torture herself any further?

Her mother's erratic, unusual behaviour troubled her. Since childhood, Gemma had learned to forgive Sue her eccentricities. Or at least to tolerate them. But this seemed different. She typed *dementia* into the search engine, and then thought some more before adding *50s*. She deleted that and put *early dementia* instead.

She didn't want results about dementia in the 1950s.

Some of the symptoms could describe her mother, but it didn't sound entirely convincing. She was shocked to read that early-onset dementia could start in someone's forties, earlier even. Could her mother really have been confused by the TV? The election? The politician?

After struggling to remember his name, Gemma typed *Hamilton Scottish Tory MP* into the search engine and clicked on the first link. The laptop screen filled with a flattering photo of Douglas Hamilton. An outdoor shot of him looking significantly less rattled than he had on the TV.

He stood tall with his cropped salt-and-pepper hair. A broad smile that never reached his eyes. His navy suit complemented with a dark rust tie. Like a politician from the eighties given a 2010 makeover.

Douglas Hamilton, the newly elected Conservative MP for Perthshire West. Majority: 2,387. Deputy chairman of the Scottish Conservatives. Retired chief inspector from Strathclyde Police. Wife. Blah, blah.

So what? Gemma knew she'd get no answers from her mother. Knew it was futile to even ask. But knew she'd ask anyway. Gemma understood from her thirty years of life that Sue wasn't a sharer. But she'd never known her to have such a visceral reaction. Ever.

As the sound of clattered dishes and gushing water came from the kitchen, Gemma reopened the window on to her dream flat. The West End. A view from the balcony of the Gothic spire of Glasgow University in the distance. Her mind drifted to when she'd walked around that campus every day, ten years before. She pulled her headphones back over her ears. Her Aretha playlist had moved on to the doleful strains of 'Until You Come Back to Me'.

CHAPTER TWO

May 1979

The fetid stench of stale urine was the first assault on the senses when descending into the Victorian public toilets on St. Vincent Street. But Jimmy had been standing at the porcelain troughs for so many hours, he could no longer smell it. Cracked mirrors above broken sinks sent the message: do your business and get out. But different people had different business there.

Jimmy stood at the urinal, looking at the fractured yellow tile in front of him, idly wondering how it had become so damaged. His brown woollen tank top with yellow spots hugged a physique that he liked to think of as a swimmer's build but was really just skinny and shapeless. The fly of his beige bell bottoms was half open and he cupped his penis in his hand. Jimmy had noticed that you saw bell bottoms a lot less these days, especially on younger guys like him.

Behind him, there was a creak from the door of one of the cubicles. It drew his attention briefly until he heard another sound. Shoes skipping down the stone steps. Jimmy's head snapped back to the fractured yellow tile.

From the corner of his eye, he saw a heavy-set man approach the urinal and glance his way. Not stout, but getting there, he wore his thick black hair combed back in a 1950s wave. He set his feet wide apart on the tiled floor and snatched another glance at Jimmy.

Jimmy could feel his heart beat faster at the sound of a zip being pulled down. A tap dripped.

Jimmy focused on the man's face, lingering more than before. As the man took out his penis, Jimmy turned his head slowly back to the yellow tile.

Wait until he shows you his penis and moves towards you. Don't show him yours first. Make eye contact only. Those were the rules.

Jimmy repeated the mantra. It was interrupted by a cough from the man, now examining Jimmy intensely. The man began tapping his left foot.

... and moves towards you. Don't show him yours first. Make eye contact...

Jimmy did. The man shuffled slightly towards him.

The heavy wooden door of the cubicle behind them crashed into the tiled wall as it swung open. An officer in the dark uniform of Strathclyde Police lunged towards the shocked man standing beside Jimmy.

'Right you, you're under arrest,' he barked. Jimmy shuffled backwards, his eyes surveying the unfolding scene. He was confused by the speed of events too.

The door of the janitor's room burst open. Out strutted a powerfully built, towering figure in the same uniform but wearing it like a king wears a royal robe. With his swinging gait, he reached the urinals in seconds and, in that time, everyone else had frozen. A smaller constable scurried behind.

Jimmy was repelled, his eyes downcast. Not for the first time in these toilets.

'Nothin' happened. You cannae touch us, Hamilton,' the urinal man sneered at the robed king, Douglas Hamilton. Jimmy stifled a snigger, taken aback by the confidence of this character.

Hamilton had been staring furiously at the policeman who'd burst from the stall. His gaze shifted robotically to the urinal man.

'That's Sergeant Hamilton to you, son.' Urinal man was at least twenty years older than Hamilton.

Jimmy's head hung low avoiding eye contact with anyone. Despite the stench, he'd happily have slid down this urinal drain to escape this moment. This place. These men.

'Mick, you've been done for importuning men in public toilets more times than I've been to Ibrox. And that's a lot. So you haud yer wheesht before ah give you a skelp,' Hamilton continued, edging closer to urinal man with every word.

'Maybe that's how ah know we didn't get close enough. You've got nothin'. We're walkin'.'

Hamilton's crack of a smile looked like it had been created by a knife slicing horizontally across his face. His deep brown eyes conveyed the message: you're in the shite, son.

'We've got four upstanding police officers who'll tell the court different.'

'This wee barra,' urinal man pointed at the officer who burst out of the cubicle, 'never saw nothin''. Confidence. Seconds. Confusion. 'Four?'

Jimmy subconsciously shuffled further back from the crime scene. His eyes met Hamilton's.

'Warren Beatty there,' Hamilton tilted his head.

Jimmy fought the feeling of his body deflating as the facts dawned on urinal man. The young policeman read his prey's every reaction as he ran the gamut in seconds: realisation, anger, betrayal, disgust.

'You're a hundred times worse than these bastards,' he told Jimmy.

Jimmy believed him. He sucked in his shame and opened his mouth, uncertain what was about to escape.

'And you're nicked, pal,' Jimmy said. His heart pumped. A toxic mixture of adrenalin, fear and loathing. The trickling of water from the leaky tap was the only breach of the stillness in the room.

Hamilton clapped his meaty hands causing Jimmy to jump.

'Right, fun's over. Get your dick back in, Mick. Warren Beatty given you the script,' Hamilton said as he nodded to the short officer who'd followed him out of the janitor's office. Urinal man was handcuffed. Before he was led away, he glared at Jimmy and shook his head.

It was more in pity than hatred, Jimmy thought, but he could have been convincing himself of that. Either way felt revolting.

Hamilton turned to Jimmy. 'We'll call it a night, son.' Hamilton was only four years older than him. 'And you're nicked, pal,' he laughed, shaking his head like an indulgent father. 'Classic... you've had a good shift. You're a natural.'

Jimmy felt like a good shift was the last thing he'd had. Hamilton ruffled his hair. He stopped laughing abruptly, removed his hand and pointed into the face of the other police officer.

'As for you, bawbag. You're no on cubicle duty again. If you cannae wait until something happens before you shoot your bolt, you can sit in the jannie closet for six hours wae that stinky Paterson.' He shook his head and motioned for the crestfallen officer to follow.

Jimmy scanned the abandoned toilet as he heard the heavy pairs of shoes ascend the battered stone stairs. A sound that had echoed through the decades. He stared at himself in the cracked mirror above the broken sink. The shards distorted his thin face, leaving his eyes lopsided and his nose virtually split down the middle.

The young policeman had played his part. Always. How commendable that was, well, that was another question.

Jimmy dragged his bleary blue eyes from his shattered image in the smashed mirror. Back to the fractured yellow tile on the wall above the urinal. And he wondered how it had all got so damaged.

***

Hamilton emerged from the depths of the toilet onto the street, his lacky in toe. As he walked through the imposing black iron gates that surrounded the entrance, he turned.

'Sorry, son, I was bit hard on you there.'

'Nae worries, Hamilton. I fucked it.'

'I'll fix it,' Hamilton patted him on the back. 'It's fine when it's us, but mind call me sarge in front of the new lads.' He tilted his head towards the toilets. 'How's Karen?'

'Och, she's fine, Hamilton. Eh... sarge. Sick every morning, eh? But that's normal seemingly.'

'How long to go?'

'Due in October.'

'Sounds right.' He had no idea, but confidence always trumped knowledge.

'The boy did well, eh?' said the young PC.

'He did,' Hamilton nodded. 'If we need tae huv these wee papist poofters in the polis, we might as well put them tae some good I suppose.' Hamilton laughed and his young colleague followed. After the squalidness of hiding in the public toilets for hours on end, Hamilton found himself disorientated by the brightness of Glasgow's summer evening.

'Where's the poof we busted earlier that I told you not to put in the van with the rest of them?' The young PC looked confused. Hamilton glared at him. 'If you cannae remember a conversation from two hours ago, you're fucked as a polis. Tall skinny, gangly drip. Looked like cancer might take him any minute.'

It dawned on the young PC, and he pointed to the unmarked police car further up the street. Hamilton patted him on the back again and strode towards it. He reached the blue Ford and opened the back door, sliding inside. A man in his thirties sat crumpled beside him, shaking.

'How you doing there?'

The man nodded his bowed head. He tried to look up to Hamilton, but the burden was too great.

'I've seen you in court. Am I right?'

The man's face creased. He nodded. Hamilton revelled in his humiliation but stifled a sneer.

'I mean, I know you're not the procurator fiscal. But I've seen you with him. One of his lawyers?' The man made no movement. Hamilton leaned his head towards him. Lowered his voice. Slowed his words. 'I asked you a question.'

The man nodded. Hamilton outstretched his hand, and the man stared at it. He looked Hamilton in the eye for the first time and tentatively put forward his own hand to shake. Hamilton grasped it and put his middle finger slightly higher so that it stroked the man's wrist. The man did the same.

'And what age is your granny?' Hamilton said and smiled. The man visibly relaxed.

'Two hundred and forty-six,' he responded.

'Mine is forty-four,' Hamilton said.

It was the orange order code. What age is your granny meant what number was your orange lodge. The man started to breathe again. A mason and an orangeman. Talk about insurance. He lifted his shoulders, a hope of reprieve.

'Who's at home? Wife?' Hamilton asked, gently.

The man nodded.

'Kids?' Hamilton said, an affected air of sympathy. There was no response. The man's tension had returned. Hamilton waited, he'd played this game many times before and knew he'd already won. The man eventually nodded. 'What's your wife's name?'

'Mary.'

'And the kids?' The man looked at him, baffled. Hamilton raised his eyebrows and nodded encouragingly. Solicit every detail.

'William junior and,' the man coughed his discomfort, 'Graeme'.

'Mary, William junior and Graeme,' Hamilton repeated, more for his own memory than anything. He shuffled aside and pulled his small black notebook from his back pocket. He passed it to the man with a pen. 'Write your name and address here.'

The man hesitated then took the pen, still suspicious. He wrote down the details.

'Mind write down the information I asked for. Best handwriting. I don't want to have to bump into you in court to clarify it.'

The man scrubbed something out in the notepad and wrote again. When he finished, Hamilton took the notepad from him and squinted at it in the dimmed light.

'William Forsythe. Christ, you've got your very own Forsythe Saga going on tonight, haven't you?' Hamilton chortled at his own wit. William didn't share in the mirth.

'That's a nice part of town you're in there.' Hamilton smiled. 'Nice to know you.' He put the notebook back in his pocket and stared out of the windscreen as though considering his next move. It was all theatre. 'It's good to know people, would you agree, William?' The man nodded uncertainly. 'We all mistakes.' Hamilton inclined his head back towards the toilet entrance. 'I mean, no that. What you lot get up to in there is fucking disgusting.'

William's face exploded red with humiliation. Exactly what Hamilton had been hoping for. 'But... the rest of us make other types of mistakes from time to time is what I'm saying to you. Less sordid obviously.' He waved his hand to show his more general point. 'Would you agree, William?'

The man nodded. 'Och, you and I are going to get along swimmingly, I can see it now. Let's get you back to Mary, William junior and wee Graeme,' Hamilton said with his knife-slash smile. The man breathed with a relief that Hamilton knew would be short-lived.

'Away you go for now.' Hamilton, his smile replaced by his default scowl, slapped his burly hand on the man's leg. 'But we'll talk soon... son.'

CHAPTER THREE

May 1979

Hamilton stood in the empty office at Pitt Street police station engrossed in the TV as an earlier clip played again.

'Her Majesty, the Queen, has asked me to form a new administration.' Britain's first woman prime minister, Margaret Thatcher, stood on the steps of 10 Downing Street, surrounded by a trio of tall, flat capped police officers with immaculately knotted ties. Her cobalt suit complemented her blue eyes. Her bouffant blonde hair was lacquered into submission. The jostled camera crept toward her. Down the street, the braying crowd registered their horror and fury. 'And I would just like to remember some words of St. Francis of Assisi.' The crowd's boos became louder, more belligerent. 'Where there is discord, may we bring harmony,' she said, apparently oblivious to the rancorous noises off screen. Thatcher glanced down to read what came next in the prayer.

Hamilton chortled. 'You tell them, Maggie hen. We'll bring the fucking harmony all right. Whether the riff raff like it or not. We'll enforce the shite out of harmony for you.' He picked his flat police cap off his desk and put it on, still watching the TV. Hamilton wiped down his uniform jacket, snapping off a stray thread and wiping away some lint.

The clip of Thatcher had been replaced by the Canadian drawl of an ageing male analyst who pointed out that 'she has disappointed many feminists; as she appears to have appointed people entirely on merit, there are very few women there'.

Hamilton laughed again. 'Quite right, Maggie. One's enough.' He shook his head to himself as he turned and made his way out the door. He marched along the corridor, cap firmly placed under his arm.

Hamilton knocked once and quickly entered the office, hoping to find the inhabitant up to no good.

The DCI's bald head was down, poring over some papers. The surrounding walls were decorated with folders. The room could easily belong to a harassed librarian rather than a senior police officer.

The cleaners had been on strike for a fortnight, yet somehow this office smelled like a citrus field.

'Sir,' he said. Hamilton imagined this man pottering around the room with his feather duster like Larry Grayson.

'You need to knock, Hamilton.' DCI Aitchison sighed.

'Did knock, sir.'

The DCI looked at him, 'And not answer back.' His high-pitched voice grated on Hamilton.

'Of course, sir. You asked for me?' Hamilton could feel the DCI's frustration rising. He enjoyed it when these turds thought, but couldn't be sure, that he was being insubordinate.

With his large frame, Hamilton hovered over the superior officer. His jet-black hair was slicked back like a Brylcreem advert. Hamilton believed in wearing his vanity lightly but wearing it nonetheless.

The DCI nodded to the seat across his desk, and Hamilton sat. 'I've got a new job for you and the...' the DCI searched for the least repulsive words, 'toilet team.'

'We've got good results. Sir, I think-'

The DCI waved his hand, 'Not a priority.' He searched among the files on his desk. Hamilton looked at him. He could feel the tension building in his shoulders. His fury at being dismissed by this fraction of a man. Controlled and ordered about by this over-promoted, jumped up...

Hamilton's concentration snapped back as he was handed a thin brown file. He flicked it open, hoping his contempt wasn't on display. The hierarchy grated on him when the hierarchy was full of such pathetic specimens as DCI Aitchison.

'I want you to lead an undercover team. A bit more immersive than what you've been up to. Look into these lot. The details are in there. Various groups... eh... socialists, communists, greens... eh... save the hedges, stop the whatever. You'll be in a small team focusing on some Glasgow groups. Going into Glasgow University firstly to get introductions to more established organisation. Student bodies are more transient so possibly more trusting of newcomers. Kids rebelling against their doctor dads before they graduate and become respectable lawyers. Some such thing.' A smirk sneaked across the DCI's face. 'I suppose you'd be what they call a mature student. I'm sure you'll fit right in.'

Hamilton glanced up at the DCI, who was looking down at him from his elevated chair. Pathetic power move. Small men liked big seats.

'Who knows, maybe you'll learn something, Hamilton,' the senior officer sneered. 'I'll obviously remain in charge of the investigation. You keep me posted. Not too posted obviously. I've got better things to do than read about what some posh students are bumping their gums about in West End pubs.' He looked back at his desk.

'So, *this* is a priority, sir?'

The DCI pointed at him. 'I'd have left you in they toilets till you were drawing your pension, Hamilton.' The boss sat back in his chair, visibly annoyed with himself for letting his subordinate get to him. He tried to be breezy, but the transformation was too quick to be anything but affected. 'That said, if the powers that be want babysitters for some mouthy weans, then I could think of no more irrelevant jobs you could be fucking up.' He dismissed him with a wave of the hand. 'Just don't batter any of the wee cherubs. Their parents will be "letters to the chief constable" types.'

Hamilton rose, standing over the desk. '1979, sir. Things are changing. Glad to be keeping an eye on these radicals. Finally. Sir.' He thought of Margaret Thatcher's call to arms at the door of Downing Street. Enforcing harmony over discord. Truth over error. Time to stop pandering to these dangerous subversives. Hamilton's chest puffed out as though it was about to have a medal pinned onto it.

'Aye,' the DCI said, 'you keep telling yourself that. I'm certain you'll deliver to your usual standards.'

Hamilton stood. A lid kept firmly on all the vitriol that wanted to pour from him. 'If that's all. Sir.' He'd perfected the art of making "sir" sound like an insult.

The DCI ignored him as he picked up his cap and left the room. He charged down the corridor, his face red with fury. A young constable came towards him and nodded his head in acknowledgment, but Hamilton marched past without returning the gesture. He threw open the wooden swing doors at the end of the corridor.

His mind was charged with the humiliation he felt. His work dismissed. His reputation disrespected. Being dressed down and ordered around by this admin assistant.

He took to the stairs, descending two at a time as though en route to an emergency. His heavy black boots thundered off each step until he reached the landing.

Hamilton entered the changing room, slamming the door behind him. He paced around the empty space, his breathing shallow.

The packet of Player's Navy Cut in his inside pocket rubbed against his chest. He took the box out and lit a cigarette. The smoke filled his lungs, the nicotine a balm for his bruised pride.

'Prick,' he said, as he inhaled deeper. He took the cigarette from his lips and glanced at the police cap that sat beside him. Attached to the black felt above the Sillitoe tartan - the distinctive chequered band - was a metal badge emblazoned with the crest of Strathclyde Police. A merged force, still in its infancy, imposing its authority over half the country. The thistle, surrounded by its leaves, was bedecked with a crown. Its motto: *Semper Vigilo. Always Vigilant.*

Hamilton took the lit cigarette from his mouth and crushed it out on the badge of the cap. Embers fell to the ground as the metal blackened. He dropped the butt on the floor and nodded in satisfaction as he crushed it underfoot.

ELAINE RUBY

Elaine Ruby is a freelance translator from Ireland. Having read crime fiction from a young age, she discovered her passion for travel and foreign cultures while working for an airline in Germany. She now divides her time between Cork and Madrid. *At Sea in Madrid* is her first novel.

elaine.noelle.ruby@gmail.com

At Sea in Madrid

The opening of a novel

CHAPTER ONE

Not another bloody letter. Who the hell were Synchronicity? It was the second one he'd got in a week. He'd binned the first letter after a cursory glance, as it had been addressed to the occupant of apartment 8B. Although surprising that it was in English, it still looked like junk mail. Probably from some expat yoga group of an AllNations acquaintance. He'd been too busy lately to go to their events. Someone from AllNations was probably trying to lure him back into the expat fold with a gym deal.

Whatever claptrap Synchronicity was trying to peddle, Adam wasn't interested. He'd enough on his plate. The purchase had finally gone through. As much as he loved the Spanish way of life, and how they lived in the moment, they made an art form out of stretching any bureaucratic process to the limit. It wasn't the only thing at its limit. He was feeling very close to it too. The Spanish weren't listening when Benjamin Franklin said, 'Don't put off until tomorrow what you can do today'. There was no point in being impatient at this stage. He finally had one foot on the Spanish property ladder, and he intended to embrace the fact that he was a homeowner. Even if it was in name only.

He glanced again at the second letter. It too was in a green envelope with the now familiar Synchronicity stamp. However, this time it was addressed to him personally. Ripping it open with a frown, he saw that it contained a single green sheet. The stationery and stamp all looked so eco-friendly and innocuous. However, skimming the content made him think otherwise. Although crafted to sound like an ordinary invitation, something seemed to be lurking behind the bland words. He read it twice in case he was being overly suspicious, but his gut reaction remained the same. The jaunty tone rang hollow.

Dear Adam,

Congratulations on getting a foothold on the Spanish property ladder! We at Synchronicity are delighted that you accepted free membership of our exclusive club of property owners. We meet weekly to discuss potential projects and share experiences of owning property in Madrid. Our next meeting will be at eight on Thursday evening (1 December) in Room 301 in Calle Carretas 20, and we sincerely hope you will join us. As we are aware that owning property in a foreign country may seem daunting at first, we would like to guide you along this exciting new path. We feel sure that we can assist you in navigating the complexities of Spanish property ownership so that you can maximise the associated benefits. As it will be both a networking and social occasion, we will be providing wine and tapas.

We are confident that it is in your interest to attend, and we are looking forward to meeting you and making future plans.
Kind regards,
Juana Pérez

He was about to bin this letter when something in the bottom right corner caught his eye. A scanned copy of his signature. How on earth did they get his signature? It was surreal. He wasn't much of a gym person, which didn't matter anyway, as this exclusive club didn't appear to have anything to do with downward dogs or sun salutations. He hadn't signed up for any new clubs either, as he'd barely enough time as it was.

Adam glanced at the uninviting green invitation again. Even the flimsy page seemed to weigh more now than it did when he first took it out of the envelope. Juana's English seemed very good, but she probably hadn't composed it herself. She hadn't used Google Translate or any other crap machine translation program either by the sound of her carefully worded message. Whoever it was, he needed to know. They could use his signature for anything. Adam felt the same vulnerability that one feels as a foreigner living in another country where the spoken language is not one's mother tongue. Regardless of how well he spoke the language, there was always scope for doubt as to his knowledge of all the written and unwritten rules and regulations that impinge on daily life. There never seemed to be any shortage of international scams either.

Adam fumbled in his pocket for his mobile and googled *Synchronicity*. His search returned numerous websites about the Swiss psychiatrist and psychoanalyst Carl Jung who coined the term, as well as several websites referencing the last album released by The Police. There was only one website that appeared to be a likely candidate for Adam's new club. *Synchronicity Property Association* (*SPA*) was emblazoned against a crimson background with the symbol of Madrid, the familiar bear leaning against a strawberry tree, tucked into the far corner of the homepage. Clicking on the various links led him to generic photos of penthouse apartments in Salamanca, studios in Chueca and new duplexes under construction on the former grounds of Atlético de Madrid's Vicente Calderón stadium and marketing fluff about property management and owners' advice forums. Synchronicity had included a menu in English on their website, so Adam was able to skim through their scant offering. It seemed like any bog-standard website that was trying to convince visitors of their need for the goods or services on offer. When he clicked on the *Contact Us* link, an elaborate video showing clips of beautiful buildings in Madrid flashed across his screen accompanied by a husky voice that said, 'You don't need to contact us because we'll contact you.' *What the fuck?*

Adam checked the time of the meeting again. The green invitation was becoming increasingly grubby in his sweaty hands. It said next Thursday. Paloma's birthday. He was invited to Museo Chicote for cocktails with Paloma, her brother Victor, and her parents at eight, followed by dinner on the rooftop terrace of Bellas Artes. He couldn't possibly tell Paloma that he'd arrive later because he had a meeting at a club he had never even joined. If he told her everything, she'd tell him to chill out and ignore the letter. 'Life's too short for worrying' was her motto. It's easy to be carefree when the Bank of Daddy was permanently open with interest-free loans and no repayment terms. Adam was convinced that Paloma's overbearing father Ramon used his wealth to keep his only daughter dependent on him.

Stuffing the cryptic invitation into his rucksack, Adam was glad to see the lift waiting to whisk him up to his eighth-floor apartment. He never took the lift for granted. Tenants on lower floors were often too careless to close the lift's door after them, and the lift idled on their floor. Their thoughtlessness riled Adam, especially as it was usually the seventh-floor tenants who were the culprits. Adam never felt like walking seven flights of stairs after a long day at the Retiro Language School.

On reaching his apartment, however, he tended to forget the effort it had taken to get there. Although even the rental agency admitted that his home was compact, his snug sitting room opened out on to a balcony with a glorious view extending south over Madrid's red rooftops all the way to the distant Cerro de los Ángeles, considered the geographic centre of the Iberian Peninsula. Translated as the Hill of the Angels, it always reminded him of the popular phrase *'De Madrid al cielo'* meaning 'From Madrid to heaven', by which locals proudly proclaimed that after seeing Madrid, only heaven was the next best thing. Having fallen in love with the city when he moved there in 2018, Adam was inclined to agree.

Closing his apartment door, Adam made a beeline for the kitchen. Extracting a chilled bottle of *Mahou* from his almost empty fridge, he headed for the balcony to drink his beer while admiring the sunset. It always felt like the most relaxing way to unwind after a long day of teaching and talking. Although he had intended to complete his application form for the school's Assistant Director role that evening, he didn't feel like doing it. The application had to be submitted by Friday, but he suspected that he was the favoured candidate.

He had been walking to class earlier that day when he had heard the familiar squeak coming up behind him. The school's Director, Fernando, had a convenient habit of wearing leather shoes that heralded his arrival before he appeared. He would never have caught any staff members bitching about him because his footwear would have forewarned them of his imminent approach. Not that he gave anyone reason to criticise him. Fernando had been the school's Director for twenty years, and he was well-respected and genuinely liked by everyone. As a proud *madrileño*, he was pleased to see Adam and other foreign teachers embracing his city and the lifestyle it offered.

'I was surprised James applied for the Assistant Director position,' Fernando had said in his accent-free English, one black eyebrow raised expectantly.

'James has applied? He's only been here six months,' Adam had said without thinking.

'He's ambitious. No one can fault him for that.' An amused smile had tugged at Fernando's lips.

'I'd have thought you'd want a more mature Assistant Director. James is in his mid-twenties at most.'

'Why haven't you applied?'

'I *am* going to apply. I have until Friday, don't I?'

'You're cutting it fine. James showed initiative by applying early.'

'To be honest, I've been up to my eyes sorting out my property purchase. You know the endless red tape involved in buying a home here,' Adam had said in his defence.

'You've bought an apartment in Madrid?' Fernando hadn't concealed his surprise.

'Yes. A lovely penthouse apartment on Avenida de Menéndez Pelayo with a gorgeous rooftop terrace overlooking the Retiro.'

'Wow, well done! Most *madrileños* would give their eye teeth to live there.'

'Thanks!' Adam had said, glancing at his watch. 'Sorry, Fernando. I have a class. I'll submit my application.'

'You do that, Adam, and I'll put it to the top of the pile.' Fernando had smiled encouragingly as he'd left.

Adam had wanted to escape before Fernando grilled him on his new apartment. He had been clearly impressed by Adam's savvy purchase. He might have been less impressed if he knew that Adam was only the bare owner while his elderly usufructuary was still named on the deeds of the property and could live there until she popped her clogs.

CHAPTER TWO

By Thursday, the only thought Adam had given to the Synchronicity meeting was when he had seen the familiar green paper discarded among old supermarket receipts on his kitchen worktop that morning. Once he'd realised that he couldn't go to the meeting, he'd managed to dismiss it as a clever marketing ploy rather than anything sinister. He'd been so focused on organising Paloma's birthday present that he hadn't had time to tell her about the strange letters.

Adam would have preferred to have had Paloma all to himself on her birthday and was disappointed when she mentioned that their dinner plans included Victor and her parents. He wasn't surprised though. One of the many things he loved about the Spanish was the fact that they were so family-oriented, like the Irish. The roles would be reversed in two weeks when Adam's parents came to visit him. They would want Paloma to join them for meals and trips. It was his turn now to spend time with her family.

Although Paloma had a good job in events management, her passion lay elsewhere. She adored art, but any notions she'd had of studying art had been dismissed by her father as whimsical and far too bohemian. Adam knew he was biased but still thought her paintings were bold and beautiful, like herself. Knowing she lacked the confidence to pursue her dream, he always encouraged her. Adam knew what it was like to dream. He'd once dreamt of becoming a musician but had long since resigned himself to composing lyrics that no one else would hear.

Paloma's birthday present was wrapped and positioned by his front door, as he had been afraid that he might go to work on Thursday without it. Knowing that Paloma wanted to visit the Amalfi Coast and paint its stunning scenery, Adam had booked two Iberia tickets to Naples and an apartment in the city's Spanish Quarter for the first two nights. They could decide later whether they wanted to stay in Sorrento or Positano. Having purchased a purple satin box in Corte Inglés, he had filled it with printouts of the tickets and accommodation, a guidebook to the Amalfi Coast and a Strathmore 300 series canvas pad. He had got wrapping paper from their favourite Italian restaurant. It was only the paper they used for takeaways, but it bore jaunty pictures of scenic Italian vistas.

As Thursday was Adam's busiest day at the school, he was looking forward to finishing at seven. On encountering Fernando in the corridor at lunchtime, he had assured him that he'd submit his application on time. Since Fernando was Spanish, Adam reckoned that the new Associate Director needed to be a foreigner to convey the impression of an international school. With his seniority, any interview would be a formality.

The competition wasn't going to go down without a fight though, as Adam discovered on entering the staff room after his final class. James was sitting at the long table nibbling on a rice cake and looking his usual miserable self.

'I expect the new Associate Director will need to speak the Queen's English rather than some bastardised version,' James said through a mouthful of unappetising crumbs.

'Give it a rest. We gave the world Joyce, Wilde and Beckett.' Adam had heard it all before from James.

'The school would have far more clout if its Associate Director not only taught English but *was* actually British.'

'I imagine Fernando wants someone with experience, James.'

'Maybe, but perhaps the school needs young blood to inject life into it.' James wiped his lips.

Thinking that James himself needed some life injected into him, Adam stifled a smile while retrieving Paloma's present from his locker and slipping it into his rucksack.

'I'd have thought you'd enough to worry about, what with Brexit...'

Adam's final remark obviously hit a nerve, as James refocused on his snack and acted as if Adam wasn't there. Exiting the staffroom, Adam felt confident that it was only a matter of time before he was the new Associate Director.

CHAPTER THREE

Adam felt good as he strode up Gran Via to Museo Chicote. As a film and history buff, he loved the colourful past of the legendary art deco cocktail bar. He had read somewhere that Museo Chicote had been the preferred watering hole of Ernest Hemingway during the Spanish Civil War, as well as that of Allied and Nazi spies, smugglers, bullfighters, and film stars like Grace Kelly and Ava Gardner during the forties and fifties. Running late because he'd gone home to change, Adam glimpsed his reflection in a shop window and was glad that he'd opted to wear his new black trousers and elegant winter coat. He looked like a man who was going places.

As Adam pushed open the ornate door and stepped into the plush red velvet surroundings, he felt that he was inhaling history. The dimmed lighting created a relaxed vibe, and his taste buds were already anticipating a cocktail. Seeing Paloma in a booth in the far-right corner, Adam waved and proceeded to weave his way between the chrome tables that stood in his path. Paloma and her parents watched him approach, their half-empty cocktails in front of them.

'You finally made it,' Ramon said in his usual gruff tone.

'Happy birthday, Paloma! You look wonderful. Sorry I'm late. I went home to change.' Adam ignored Ramon's remark.

'Thanks, *cielo*.' Paloma jumped up to embrace him. She always encouraged her parents to speak English with Adam, allegedly to improve their English. However, Adam felt it was more so that he could understand everything.

'You look lovely too, Carmen.' Adam smiled at Paloma's mother. Carmen beamed appreciatively and stood up so Adam could kiss her on both cheeks, as customary in Spain.

'Good to see you, Adam.' Carmen touched his cheek with her bejewelled hand. Adam and Ramon merely nodded at each other. A double kiss was a step too far for them.

'We're having fabulous champagne cocktails!' Paloma raised her glass to her scarlet-tinted lips as Adam sat down.

'Where's Victor?' Adam asked before ordering a cocktail from a hovering barman.

'He plays *pádel* on Thursdays but will join us for dinner.' Carmen twirled the stem of her glass.

Adam admired how Paloma's black velvet dress contrasted perfectly with the swish red seating and thought she looked as stunning as any film star.

'Has your purchase been finalised?' Ramon sounded interested.

'Yes. I now own property in Madrid.' Adam couldn't hide the pride in his voice.

'Glad to hear it. Paloma deserves a man with prospects.' Ramon smiled at his daughter.

'Oooh, what's this?' Paloma squealed in delight as Adam handed her the gift bag he'd been carrying.

'I thought Adam already gave you earrings, darling,' Carmen said to his surprise.

'Earrings?' Adam glanced at both women in turn. He'd seen the look that Paloma had just shot her mother. Carmen was now staring into her glass as if she could see all seven numbers for the next *Primitiva* lottery there, while Paloma beckoned to the waiter in a clumsy attempt to change the subject. Only Ramon looked amused. After the cocktails were ordered, Adam looked expectantly at Paloma.

'Diego sent me emerald earrings for my birthday. I'd seen them years ago in Bogota airport's duty-free when we were in Columbia on holidays and regretted not buying them.'

'Your ex gave you such a personal birthday present although he knows you're my girlfriend?'

'Don't be like that, Adam. They're beautiful but don't *mean* anything. Diego and I are just friends. I want to see *your* present.' Smiling on recognising the wrapping paper, she ripped it to reveal the purple box. Opening it excitedly, her eyes fell on the travel printouts.

'Wow, Naples!!! You knew I wanted to paint the Amalfi Coast. You're the best! Thanks, *cielo*!' Leaning over, she kissed Adam's cheek, the earrings seemingly forgotten.

Their table in Azotea was booked for ten, so they strolled over to the majestic Círculo de Bellas Artes building on Calle de Alcalá after their second cocktail. On entering the lift, they were whisked up to the 7th floor with its rooftop terrace boasting one of the finest views in Madrid. Having been shown to a round table with a crisp white linen tablecloth, they were studying their menus by the flickering candlelight when Victor arrived. Adam was raging on spotting Diego with him. Who invited him?

'Look who I played *pádel* with?' Victor gestured to Diego, who looked like he'd stepped off the cover of *GQ* with his black jeans, leather jacket and Gucci man bag. Victor insisted on speaking rapidly in Spanish whenever Adam was there in an obvious attempt to exclude him.

'Happy birthday, Paloma! Victor said you wouldn't mind if I tagged along.'

'Of course not, Diego. Thanks for your gift!' Paloma said graciously, but looked uncomfortable as she shot an apologetic glance at Adam before rising for the customary kisses.

Adam remained seated, longing to punch Diego's lights out for gatecrashing. Although he wanted to leave, he suspected Ramon would relish him appearing petulant, and he couldn't spoil Paloma's birthday. He'd stay and keep a close eye on Diego who appeared to regret blowing his chance with Paloma ten years ago. With Adam's new apartment, even if in name only, and his almost certain promotion, he felt confident in his role as her man with prospects!

CHAPTER FOUR

Adam was glad it was Friday on hearing his alarm the following morning. He finished at two on Fridays and always treated himself to a leisurely *menú del día*. Although he'd lived in Madrid for four years, he still marvelled at having a lovely three-course lunch and a glass of wine for the princely sum of €12. He'd barely get the glass of wine for that price in Ireland. Adam thought about where he'd have lunch as he got dressed.

Fernando didn't impose an explicit dress code, but Adam still liked to look smart. He felt that wearing a tie looked professional and lent him a certain gravitas. Fernando was also a sharp dresser, and Adam was sure that he'd consider such things when selecting the new Associate Director. In contrast, James often looked thrown together in crumpled shirts and scruffy jeans. His sartorial inelegance wasn't a good advertisement for a private language school that claimed to be one of Madrid's best.

Adam was heading to his first class when the school secretary, Isabel, stopped him in reception.

'*Hola* Adam! I have a new group for you.' Isabel waved a scribbled note.

'Morning, Isabel. What's this?' Adam glanced at the note she'd handed him.

'I got an e-mail from a guy, Javier Torres, who owns a start-up company called GreenTech. He wants classes for himself and four employees.'

'Is this the company's address? It looks like an industrial estate in the south of Madrid, that area known for outlets selling cheap white goods.'

'Yes, it is. Señor Torres said they're searching for new premises. These are only temporary. He booked a one-hour class, but he'll book a twelve-week course if he's satisfied.'

'I'll make sure he is!'

'He specifically asked for you because he liked your profile on our website. I'll mention this to Fernando.' Isabel smiled.

'You're a star, thanks! What time is the class?' Adam was chuffed. The timing was perfect. He'd earn brownie points with Fernando for attracting clients.

'Señor Torres requested five today. I know you finish at two. Can you do it? It'll be overtime.'

'Of course, Isabel.' He could still have lunch, and then get the metro to the address. The fact that it was in an industrial estate seemed rather odd. Although he often gave classes on company premises, they were usually located in one of the high-rise glass shoeboxes in the financial district.

'I'll send you the GreenTech e-mail.'

'Great! I'll tell you on Monday how it went.' Still smiling, he headed to his class.

Adam's students were always enthusiastic on Fridays as the prospect of lunch and the expected pleasure of the weekend inched ever nearer. It never failed to amuse him how seriously the Spanish took *la comida,* the lengthy lunch invariably accompanied by drinks, and none more so than on a Friday. Adam was at the printer before his last class when he heard Fernando approaching.

'I've been looking for you. Where's your application?' Fernando frowned.

'Sorry, Fernando. I intended to submit it yesterday. I'll do it after my next class.'

'Anyone would think you weren't interested in this job, Adam.' Fernando sounded uncharacteristically irritated.

'Of course I am.'

'This isn't a one-horse race.'

'I know. I'll prove I'm the right candidate by getting a new group signed up.'

'Isabel told me about that potential client.'

'I'm just printing entrance level tests for the class.'

'I'll look forward to your update on the group. Have a good weekend!'

'You too, Fernando.'

Damn. In his annoyance about Diego muscling in on Paloma's birthday celebrations, he'd forgotten to e-mail the bloody application. All the cocktails and wine hadn't helped his memory either. He'd better buck up. Glancing at his phone, he noticed the GreenTech e-mail in his inbox. His subsequent Google search revealed that GreenTech was an innovative recycling company that intended to "make life more sustainable" according to the marketing fluff on its website. All he had to do was ensure that the twelve-week course was in the bag to make *his* life more sustainable.

CHAPTER FIVE

Adam eased himself into the plush teal seat in *Vi Cool*, his favourite restaurant for *la comida*. He had perused the *menú del día* at the entrance and fancied some *paella*. It was annoying if he chose a restaurant based on its outside menu only to subsequently discover that his desired dish was no longer available. This discovery was usually made when he was sipping his first glass of wine and had already committed to the restaurant. Having learnt from experience, he had enquired about the *paella* on approaching his table. The young waiter who knew him had laughed, baring brilliant white teeth.

'You are a real *madrileño*, Adam! You take food as seriously as we do.'

'Your food deserves to be taken seriously.'

'*Albariño?*'

'Please, and *boquerones fritos* followed by *paella*, Juan.'

'Perfect.'

Adam was soon savouring a glass of chilled *albariño* and a plate of fried anchovies while surveying the raucous lunchtime crowd. Several older ladies were squeezed around a nearby oval table exchanging gifts and squealing delightedly on discovering their contents. Some of them shot him admiring glances, making him smile. Life was good. He lived among fun-loving people, had a stunning girlfriend and a good job. And he was a homeowner to boot. The fact that he couldn't actually live there yet was a technicality. Twirling his glass, he made a silent toast to himself and his future. It seemed right, as he'd finally submitted his application. Adam was lost in thought when Juan appeared with a steaming plate of *paella*.

'At least you know that we Spanish only eat *paella* at lunchtime and not for dinner like tourists.'

'That's one of the rules that I do actually know.' Adam surveyed the *paella* with pleasure. He was glad to be dining alone, relieved that he'd swerved having lunch with Raquel. She'd also finished her classes at two and had ambushed him as he left. Mumbling some lame excuse in response to her lunch proposal, he'd fled in the opposite direction. She was one of those women who behaved differently around men, arching her back and flicking her hair and being inappropriately coquettish. He'd once made the mistake of having lunch with her, and she'd acted as if they were on a date. Never again. She was always trying to pry into his private life, while eyeing him suggestively.

'Another?' Juan asked, seeing Adam's empty glass.

'Why not? It's Friday.'

'Dessert?'

'Just a *cortado* please.'

In truth, Adam wondered if he should have a second glass of wine. He dismissed his doubts with the thought that his new students were probably already on their second or third drink over lunch themselves. He was having a substantial lunch, and another *albariño* would wash down his *paella*. He'd finish with a strong *cortado* and would be ready to tackle any class.

Feeling sated and mellow, Adam emerged from the dimly lit restaurant into a lively street scene unfolding under a brilliant blue sky. Although only a few weeks before Christmas, the winter sun shone down on shoppers laden with brightly coloured bags bulging at their seams. Weaving his way past crowded *terrazas*, Adam hastened to the metro station near Spain's Kilometre Zero in Puerto del Sol. The main square was even busier than usual with Christmas shoppers, enormous furry cartoon characters attempting to entice passers-by to part with their hard-earned cash in return for photos, and other hawkers peddling their wares. The ubiquitous lengthy queues for the giant Christmas lottery, *el gordo,* snaked around numerous corners and only added to the feverish excitement in the air.

Sidestepping crowds, Adam approached *la boca*, literally the mouth of the metro station. Once inside its bustling interior, he got on a line 1 train heading south. It was after four, but he had sufficient time to arrive at the specified address and prepare for his class. He had a compact projector with him to show a brief presentation on the school. The portable screen would have been too awkward to carry, so he'd use a white wall instead. His plan was to introduce himself, and then get everyone to introduce themselves in turn. He could gauge their level of English from their introductions. He'd then show the presentation, get them to complete the entrance test, and finally answer any questions. The one-hour class would be over before he knew it. He'd have a new group to keep Fernando happy.

And he could start enjoying the weekend.

Alighting at Las Suertes stop, Adam ascended to ground level and re-entered the address in Google Maps. The industrial estate was ten minutes away on foot. He could see the familiar blue building and yellow signage of the local branch of *Ikea* to his right, but Google Maps was sending him left in the direction of some uninviting scrubland.

Adam traversed yawning pavements cracked by the unrelenting rays of the sun and weather-beaten signs advertising businesses that were nowhere to be seen before spotting the entrance to an industrial estate up ahead. On drawing closer, his initial assessment was confirmed by an ageing yellow sign, remnants of paint clinging to the decaying wood. Polígono Industrial de Los Pájaros was barely decipherable. A well-peeled map indicated that unit thirteen was the low-slung building on the right inside the gate. If it weren't for a solitary mechanic in greasy overalls tinkering with a dilapidated-looking truck outside Autos de Pepe on the left, Adam would've thought the industrial estate was long abandoned. Was office space so hard to find in Madrid?

Pushing open the heavy reinforced steel door, Adam was almost blinded by the harsh interior lighting that illuminated a stark white table and plastic chairs. There were certainly no distractions. He'd probably only give one or two classes here, as the company was bound to find more suitable premises in Madrid.

'I see you made it.'

VAN STANLEY

Van Stanley lives in Norfolk with her wife and two cats. She has published fantasy, horror, and science fiction short stories under a pseudonym. Her writing often features neurodiverse characters. *Egg County* is her first novel.

eggcounty@outlook.com

Egg County

The opening of a novel

CHAPTER ONE

The world was quiet out by the lake. It would have been silent if it weren't for the flies. They crawled over the picnic, half-eaten, still laid out on the table. Their thick black legs ran rampant as they gorged themselves.

The boy sat at the low bench, his hands in his lap, his eyes following one fat fly as it landed on the edge of the bowl of half-eaten chicken salad. No onions or tomatoes and with a dash of mustard in the mayonnaise, just how he liked it. His ma had made it special for his date. His eyes followed the fly to the empty foil plate which had housed the pie the girl had brought with her. Chocolate and marshmallow. The pastry, she'd told him, had been store-bought but she had done the filling. God she'd smiled so proudly when she'd told him that, the smile slipping into a grin when he assured her it was the best chocolate and marshmallow pie he had ever eaten. She'd thanked him, her eyes twinkling. Her cheeks had dimples in them.

After a time, she stood up, smoothing down the front of her skirt. Dark denim, like the jacket she liked to wear at church meets. She'd left the jacket at home at her ma's insistence. It was too hot for it. The sweltering summer heat that had dogged Egg County since mid-April had still not let up.

I need the bathroom, she had announced. He had blurted back, there ain't no restrooms, and she had laughed. Throwing her head back like it was the funniest thing she had heard all day, her long honey-blonde hair cascading down her back. She leaned down and kissed him on the cheek, her lips sticky from her lip gloss. A pearly rose-tinted shade that she wore every day without fail. It smelt of bubblegum. I know, I've hiked before, she assured him as she headed over to the bushes, she pushed one aside.

CHAPTER TWO

The night before, Nelson had agreed to take James on patrol with him. Truth be told, he didn't mind the kid. Not that Nelson thought of him as a kid, but that was how he'd come to be known at the sheriff's office.

There were only four years separating them. Four years and a college degree because while Nelson had joined the department weeks after graduating high school, James had been sent upstate by his parents. The consequences of a split condom having dictated Nelson's path for him. The way James had told it, his parents had wanted him to go into teaching. Something of a family business apparently. His grandfather had been the principal at an elementary school the far side of the city. His ma had been a teacher before she'd settled down too. She'd met James's pa in the teacher's lounge on her first day and they'd been inseparable since. His pa, it turned out, had been a gym teacher until a heart attack had hit him mid speech in the changing rooms. It had forced him to retire, leaving him to coach a community team on Fridays. The way James had told it, he'd been quite the basketball player back in the day but somehow had never struck out beyond teaching the game to kids with less talent than he'd had.

James, it turned out, had inherited neither his ma's inclination towards teaching thirteen-year-olds algebra nor his pa's athletic abilities. He'd inherited the height but none of the lankiness. He was a stocky, uncoordinated mess who looked like he had been stitched together out of spare parts. A clumsy and nice natured bull in a china shop who could tread as careful as anything but still end up smashing the place to smithereens while the proprietor watched on in horror.

To Nelson, it seemed just about everyone else at the sheriff's department minded the kid. Or at least, they minded his mouth. He always had a smart comment dancing about on his tongue and lacked the grace to swallow them. His face wasn't much help either. All pointed weasel-like features. It didn't match the rest of him. Nelson didn't mind James, sure, truth be told he'd come to think of the kid as a friend, but he could see the appeal in hating him.

There were advantages to buddying up with James though. Advantages Nelson didn't mind. The kid always paid for coffee. Breakfast too if it was the week their pay checks hit. So long as they made their way to Sparks to order it. Which was fine with Nelson. They served some of the best homemade sausage he'd ever tasted. The secret ingredient, according to the blue-eyed waitress James was so fond of, was a dash of garlic salt. Judging from his breath afterwards, Nelson had always assumed a dash meant half a cup at the very least.

'I don't understand why you don't ask her,' Nelson said as he wound the window down. It was October, but there was no chill in the air. It was thick, muggy. The mercury was still clinging to the nineties. It had been that way since April, as though the world hadn't got the memo that summer had ended. It was meant to have been swallowed up by fall at least a month back. The radio had hinted a stormfront was going to be moving in soon. A bead of sweat trickled down Nelson's neck. It couldn't come soon enough. He was a creature of cold. Maybe his brother had the right idea. He'd packed up his crummy Southside apartment and made his way north three years back. Nelson had thought about packing up and following him. He might have if it hadn't been for Sam and Juno. Not that Sam had time for him these days.

'Well, I mean for starters I think she's married,' James said pointedly. She. Mary Anne. That was with no dash. Or so James had reliably informed him. They'd gone to the same high school. She'd been the grade above him, but they'd played alongside one another in band. He was a trumpet player, while she was trombone. Or French horn. Or possibly tuba. Nelson couldn't recall. James's adoration had been born in the brass section and had dogged him ever since. Now it culminated in almost daily visits to the shitty tin-roofed diner she worked at in the hopes she was on the same shift pattern as him. Nine times out of ten she was. Nelson wondered if she lived in the place. Maybe she slept in the office or at one of the booths. Either way, it was a story for the grandkids. Or would be if James would tell her how he felt. Much better than Nelson's, if Sam or Juno ever gave him any. A one-night stand with a girl he met at a dive bar when he was eighteen. Still a high school senior, in possession of his brother's ID. The resemblance had been just enough to get him in so long as the bouncer didn't squint. He'd brought her a mojito. The bar had used basil instead of mint. The girl had drunk it anyway and had asked for another. They'd ended up getting married after graduation. But only because his ma had made him do right by her. And because he was scared of her pa. A girl who, in the end, hadn't been right for him. He hadn't blamed Amber for walking. He was just glad she let him still see Juno one weekend in every four. Even if he did have to beg his ma to drive out to pick her up for him. It was just a shame Sam never wanted to join them. It didn't matter how much his ma insisted it was just his age, Nelson knew the truth. His son hated him. He'd written as much in his last Father's Day card.

Nelson shook his head and took a sip of his still too hot coffee. He winced. It was way too sweet. They might have done the best sausage in the county, but the coffee at Sparks left a lot to be desired. It always left blisters in your mouth and came loaded with sugar by default.

'Besides,' James carried on, 'I don't think it's right to ask that. Not when she's working.'

'Yeah, you'd hate for her to think you're a creep or something, going in there nearly every day just to talk to her.' Nelson turned to stare out his window at the empty parking lot. There were four cars scattered through it. Five if you counted their busted-up cruiser, still showing the aftermath of the buck James had crashed into on his first week of the job. All of the cars belonged to the staff of Sparks. It was open twenty-four hours save for Sunday. How they turned any kind of profit was beyond Nelson, it seemed like him and James were the only customers whenever they pulled in. There were rumours. All sorts of things from drug dealing to high stakes poker. Any money laundering front you could think of had been floated about the place. Nelson took another sip of coffee and forced himself to swallow. Next time he was going to brave the tea and pray it was at least halfway palatable.

'I go in for breakfast, seeing her is just an added bonus.'

'I'm sure that's exactly what she thinks when she catches you staring at her while you eat your eggs.'

James's protest was cut off by static on the radio. Beneath it they could just make out the voice of Gem crackling into life, the static making it sound like she smoked ninety a day as opposed to her customary just shy of fifty.

'We got reports of a missing kid out near Belvedere,' Gem croaked. 'Any units near there?'

Nelson glanced at James. It had just gone six. Their shift was due to end in fifty-seven minutes. The same thought danced across their respective lips. They could lie. They could tell Gem they were up at Coal Springs dealing with a little shit who was speeding. If they were pressed, it was easy to tell another little white lie. Say they let them off with a warning. That Christmas had come early for the driver.

They could lie, but Gem would see right through it. Gem knew them. Knew them better than their own mothers ever had. She knew that near enough every shift found them at the same shitty tin-roofed diner on one of the county roads north of Belvedere. Unless it was a Sunday of course.

Nelson reached for the radio. He hesitated before transmitting.

'Can't they wait and send someone else?' James asked. He spoke in hushed tones, as though Gem could hear them without Nelson pushing the button. 'Chances are it's a runaway.'

'Do you want to ask her that?' Nelson asked. James withered at the question. Of course not. Nobody, except maybe Ramos, would ever talk back to Gem. Her tongue was a weapon, and no one willingly went up against it. Nelson pushed the button to transmit.

'This is Nelson. James and I are five, maybe ten minutes out. Give us the address and we'll head there now.'

James reached into his chest pocket and pulled out his cell phone, a Nokia which clicked anytime he hit one of the buttons.

'Your ma?' Nelson asked him.

'Just letting her know I'll be late,' James explained.

Gem crackled back into life. Nelson could hear the smile in her voice, he was thankful she had stopped him having to dwell on James's domestic situation. The kid was a real momma's boy. To the point that it made Nelson, a self-confessed momma's boy, worry for him. He'd read somewhere that serial killers often had domineering mothers. Though he doubted James could carry out something like that. He had once expressed guilt when he'd trod on a caterpillar. Ramos's voice chimed in his head, that boy ain't right.

'Knew you boys would be nearby. It's a house on Bracken. Little dead end by the looks of the map. Looks like it ain't too far from the highway. You know it?'

Nelson glanced at James who sat arms crossed and pouting like a five-year-old weighing up the merits of throwing a tantrum.

'You know it?' He repeated, the question was entirely pointless. Nelson already knew the answer. James was a fucking atlas. There wasn't a place in the entire county that he didn't know. Had he had a knack for teaching, Nelson had no doubt James would teach geography.

'Sure, I had a cousin live near there once.'

Nelson felt his eyes roll. Of course. James was an atlas. An atlas with a family tree so big it was a forest in itself.

'Is that why you haven't asked her out?' Nelson asked as he pulled out of their spot.

James gave him a quizzical look, one strawberry-blonde eyebrow raised.

'Is she secretly your cousin too?'

'Fuck you.'

CHAPTER THREE

Small stones rained upwards along the undercarriage, the asphalt having given way to a loose packed dirt track. As always, James was ready with an explanation.

'There used to be an old guy who would pay each year or so to get it resurfaced. Passed on maybe twenty years back. His son lives there now but won't pay up. Reckon the neighbours owe him for it.'

'Judging by the houses, they likely do,' Nelson said. It was a nice street, nicer than the ones he had grown up on. Around half a dozen sizable houses with manicured lawns. There was the odd weed poking its way through a crack in a path or a handful of flowers that were wilted, finding themselves on death's door after a long, hot summer. The few trees were still green for the most part, somehow thriving in the sun, though some had started to turn amber. The orange leaves marbled throughout the green, the memo fall had come finally reaching them. The cars on the drives were well cared for, paintwork shining in the early morning light. And it wasn't just one car. Every other house seemed to have two parked out front, nose to ass. Nelson squinted at each mailbox they passed. Slowing to a stop he asked, 'Can you make out the name on that mailbox?'

'Hampy. Though that A has peeled in an unfortunate place.'

Nelson killed the engine.

'This is it?' James asked.

'This is it. Do me a favour?'

'Sure.'

'Don't mention the mailbox.'

'You got it.'

A red-faced woman was outside before Nelson had slammed the door of the cruiser shut. She was a large woman, her blonde hair scraped back into a tight ponytail sitting high on her head. She was wearing a floral nightgown with a pair of pantyhose, a hole at the knee.

'You're finally here,' she had a shrill way of speaking. Her slippered feet hung over the edge of the stoop. 'I was getting dressed… I was going to drive down to the station to talk… I…'

Finally. The word needled at Nelson. Like he and James hadn't made the seven-minute drive in three minutes, lights flashing while they were on the highway, risking waking the fine folk of Belvedere. A shitty move so early in the morning, especially on a Saturday when people were trying to catch a lie-in instead of having to turn out on the freeway to whichever office, hospital or factory helped to pay the mortgage, put food on the table, and keep the shiny cars out front. Finally. That word always found itself in someone's mouth. Finally.

'We came as quick as we could.' Nelson said with a smile. It was forced but if he'd learned anything bagging groceries as a kid, it was that playing along stopped you being the one called into the manager's office at the end of your shift. If he smiled while in uniform, there was less chance he'd be called into Ramos's office next time he clocked in. Ramos loved drilling in the importance of community. Especially when it came to the good folk of Belvedere. They were the type who would buy into her campaign when she made her bid for sheriff official, which would be any day now the news about Lawes was out and she'd been given the caretaker role. Shot on duty, now coming off life support, a heroic end. The governor had made a statement about mourning, Ramos would fill in until the funeral, and then they'd announce an election. They'd keep the dirty details out of the press. Keep things clean for the governor. It was easier for the folk around here to think of Lawes as a hero.

'I'm Officer Nelson,' he held out a hand, convinced she'd slap it away. James had been a Belvedere boy, even if only by association. Nelson had grown up on the fringes of The Yolk; he'd grown up poor. He'd never quite shook the thought people could smell it on him. The lingering stink of the deprivation. Like somehow, he still smelt of his pa's menthols and cheap fabric softener.

The woman reached out. Her hand felt surprisingly callused. Not the soft, lower middle class hand Nelson had expected. Up close, Nelson could see how bleary her eyes were, could see the tell-tale silver slime trails on the sleeve of her nightgown where she'd been wiping her nose while she waited. A mother just about holding it together. Nelson pulled his hand free and placed it in his pants pocket, wiping his fingers on the stiff cotton. He'd never quite shook the urge to wash his hand when he met someone for the first time.

'I know who you are. You live near my brother.'

Nelson studied the woman's face. He couldn't place her. But this was Egg County. It was small. He hoped this branch of the family tree was a little more civilised, or else he and James might need to radio Gem for backup.

'We able to talk inside?'

CHAPTER FOUR

The house was tired inside, in desperate need of a lick of paint, but it wasn't an unloving house. As Nelson followed the woman down the hall into the kitchen, he clocked family photos on just about every available surface. A sunburnt, smiling trio with Mickey Mouse on an end table at the foot of the stairs. A baby, laughing, on an old woman's lap who was grinning and revealing rows of missing teeth. A family portrait hung on the wall by the door to the kitchen, a blonde girl in a denim jacket was shouting unheard words from inside the frame, a church standing proudly behind them.

Nelson stepped over a scattering of green plastic soldiers, a battalion steadfastly guarding the basement stairs. The woman uttered a flustered apology. She had no idea what they were doing there. She'd asked Anthony to clean them up after his friend Joey had left last night. God, she was babbling. She apologised.

Nelson and James sat themselves at the kitchen table. James took a pocketbook out and waited, pen poised. They had practised this routine many times now. Nelson would talk, and James would take notes. Then when they handed a case over, they weren't hassled for the small details. Ramos loved hassling people for the small details. Especially, it seemed, when they were missing.

Nelson broke the silence. His voice was warm, friendly. It was rehearsed. False. His public voice. 'I didn't catch your name outside.'

'Emily Harbour.'

Emily Harbour stood by the stove, a great hulking thing in a cheery yellow colour. She was rocking on the balls of her feet while wringing her hands. She was actually wringing them like an anxious school kid about to catch a whooping off their ma for being caught trying to forge their report card to hide the fact they'd failed Math again.

'Not Hampy?' James asked.

'Hampy was my mother's name.' Emily's sniffling did not conceal the coldness in her voice. 'She passed last fall, but I don't see what that has to do with anything.'

'We just need all the details, ma'am.' Nelson ignored the alarm bells the name had set off in his head. It was just his luck that she was related to Billy Hampy. Would they have to question him? Would they find him in the drunk tank in Arlis or King County? Or would he be at home? Nelson hoped for the former. He didn't want Billy to give him a hiding for knocking on the door.

'Of course, of course. Whatever I can do to help.'

'It's appreciated. I know this must be hard. We've been told your daughter didn't come home last night.' It was a statement, not a question, and it made the poor woman crumple like a paper doll. She tried to speak but just sobbed, and shook her head, burying her blotchy red face in her chubby tanned hands.

James opened his mouth again. Nelson kicked him under the table. A quick but not insignificant blow that said shut the fuck up. That he was on mighty fucking thin ice. It wasn't that James was a bad person. Nelson had worked with him enough to have figured out he didn't have a bad bone in his body. Not really. Not where it counted. He just seemed to lack the ability to read the room at every wrong moment. It would be better for everyone if he kept it buttoned up, truth be told. James closed his mouth. Nelson was thankful, as ever, that the kid was at least capable of taking a hint.

'What's your daughter's name?' Nelson asked.

'Ren.'

'Wren as in the bird?'

'No. Ren. It's short for Lauren. We named her for my sister. She passed when she was twelve.'

'Well, you have my condolences. That can't have been an easy thing to go through. And how old is Ren? Your Ren I mean.'

'Sixteen.'

James opened his mouth again. Nelson didn't react in time, he flinched as the words tumbled out of the younger man's mouth.

'Are you sure she's not a runaway?'

Nelson closed his eyes. One of Emily's heaving great sobs filling his ears. He could feel his soul sinking. Straight down to hell. He could feel the flames dancing round his ankles. His punishment for buddying up with James.

CHAPTER FIVE

'I fucked that up, didn't I?' James asked. The didn't I came out like one jumbled up word. Dinteye.

Nelson didn't answer. He just kept his eyes forward, swerving to avoid a white-tailed buck stood at the edge of the road.

James sighed. 'Look, I know I fucked up.'

'Then why did you ask the damn question?' Nelson asked. There was no anger in his voice. No malice. Just weariness.

It had taken him a good ten minutes to calm Emily Harbour down and finish getting what they needed. He'd sent James outside to sit in the cruiser. He'd been frightened Emily might whoop him with the large, cast-iron frying pan that had been sitting on her stove top. The poor woman had turned hysterical. Not that Nelson could blame her. Like it or not, he'd have done the same. Ren, it turned out, wasn't right. Those weren't Nelson's words, but her ma's. She weren't like other girls. She was wired different. God bless her. Nelson had ended up pouring Emily a mug of coffee from the pot she'd had brewing at the outlet by her fridge to get her to settle down enough for him to learn what he'd needed to learn. That Ren was in special ed classes. That she had a boyfriend. That she'd gone on a date with him the night before. That she hadn't come home from said date. Nelson sighed and relayed what he knew to James.

'We headed to the boyfriend's?' James asked.

Nelson gave him a stiff nod.

'Where does he live?'

'Arlis.' Nelson's eyes didn't move from the road. He didn't need to look at James to know his eyes would be bulging. He was a stickler for procedure, and sure as the sky was blue piped up asking why they were straying out of Egg County.

'That Arlis P.D's jurisdiction, ain't it?' he added, emphasising the word jurisdiction.

'They won't care. Not about just popping in to check for a girl who's probably at her boyfriend's for some reason. They might have just lost track of time or… innocently fallen asleep or something.'

'Did she try calling his house?'

'No landline apparently.'

'If Ramos finds out…'

'Ramos won't give a shit, James. Like she doesn't give a shit if Arlis P.D come out into the sticks to haul in someone who was shoplifting at the mall on Southside.' Strictly speaking, that wasn't true. If Ramos found out Nelson had slipped into the city in his cruiser to look for a missing girl without making a scene, she'd understand the judgement call. If one of theirs came into one of their unincorporated communities to serve a warrant without radioing and asking for one of theirs to be present, Ramos would shit the bed. It was a double standard, sure, but that was Ramos all over. The woman was a walking, talking double standard. Though she'd make your life hell if you made a point of saying as such.

JESSICA TOSELAND

Jessica Toseland grew up in semi-rural West Yorkshire, taking inspiration from the temperamental weather and dramatic landscape. Her first novel adapts Gothic tropes for the modern day, exploring themes of confinement, isolation and horror – specifically in dialogue with destructive gender relations and human greed.

jesstoseland00@gmail.com

Bodies at the Crown

The opening of a novel

PROLOGUE

I'm standing with my shoes off and Peter lying at my feet.

I'm onstage in the hotel ballroom, bare soles against polished wood. Grainy dots appear in front of my eyes and I think I'm going to black out again. Then the spots clear and I'm able to take everything in.

Peter's face is grey, skin stretched taut over immobile muscle; his mouth hangs slack with what looks like surprise. He could be having a fit, but something tells me he's much too still. I don't want to touch him, but I kneel anyway to check for a pulse. I can't find one on his wrist or his neck.

Something has led you here. Something has led you to this point.

The voice from my dreams is back; I try to ignore it. There's blood, slowly pooling from the back of his head.

Who could be to blame?

I look around; there's no-one else here. Shock and nausea seize me and I almost wish for my unconsciousness back, but now I'm wide awake. Breathe. Think clearly, think logically. How could this have happened?

You never thought you'd see him like this, did you? Rolled onto his back like a dog awaiting a belly rub.

Perhaps part of you enjoys it.

There's a gap in the lighting rig above my head. A stage light is missing. It could have fallen and struck Peter on the head. Unless someone purposely detached it. The light is nowhere to be seen.

Peter's speech. I check the time: ten minutes to nine. Ten minutes until the servers will prop open the doors to the ballroom and guests will flood the hall. Adrenalin rushes me and I go light-headed. The lines of Peter's suit trousers are still crisp and precise.

I didn't do this; I know in my body I didn't do this. I have to get out of here.

Back away from Peter, towards the wings. Maybe I can wait out the night in there; can't be seen coming out of the ballroom, not now. My back makes contact with something solid – hands grab hold of my elbows. I barely stifle a scream before twisting round.

'Ros?' says Julian. He looks down. 'You're not wearing any shoes.'

'Julian,' I say, terror gripping my throat; he'll suspect me immediately. 'I don't know – I just got here but I don't –'

'It's alright,' he says, looking past me, looking at Peter. His hand begins stroking down my arm and I fight the urge to recoil. 'It's alright.'

I see the recognition of power lighting up his eyes, recognition of my sudden weakness.

Careful, now – this is just the opportunity he's been waiting for.

'I can help you,' he says.

CHAPTER ONE
Four Days Earlier

Beyond the windows the sun is gone. My eyes flit to the bottom right corner of my computer screen. It's only five o'clock. Days are short in winter. Leaded windows make the entry room feel smaller than it is. The darkness outside is flat, two-dimensional, making the hotel feel like the only real place on earth.

I'm backed on all sides by crimson, papered walls. Striped vertically red and burgundy, with a little indented crown motif repeated over and over. The floorboards are polished oak, scuffed by countless boot marks and suitcase wheels. A faded antique rug runs from the main entrance to the front desk, where I sit. Behind me is a glass-panelled door that leads into Julian's office, which protrudes from the back wall. The front desk is a semi-circle of polished, dark-red wood, imitating mahogany.

I never thought I'd work here this long, but the truth is I've nowhere else to go. After Nan passed and her house was repossessed, I was out on my own. Peter offered me one of the unused rooms at the top of the hotel, minimal rent.

I owe Peter a lot. That doesn't mean I have to like him.

The hotel itself I do like. The Crown balances precariously on the edge of a cliff. For centuries it's been a landmark destination, the only thing the village of Crosswich is known for. I know some history: the castle was originally built as a reward from Henry VIII to some favoured lord or other. The hotel underwent restoration during the nineteenth century, officially opening in 1844.

Over the years I imagine many owners have tried to imprint themselves on it. But I like to think the essence, the ragged touch of the walls and the baleful shriek of the wind, remains the same. Feverish in summer and deathly cold in winter. Since I've worked here no-one can ever seem to get the temperature right.

I think about the bones of the building, whether resentment accumulates there. Handed from man to man, not only watching but feeling yourself change to accommodate their grand visions – before they leave and the cycle begins anew.

Does bitterness linger in the walls? Surely it must.

Wall lights are dimmed low, casting an orange glow over the portraits hung at intervals. Gaunt, medieval faces loom out of black backdrops. There's a young woman next to me – I can read her name, the year she died. I can see the individual brush strokes that compose her liquid face, and the individual strokes of the darkness behind her.

I imagine a portrait of myself hanging there; with my screen-tired eyes it's easy to superimpose my own features over the young woman's. I see myself as a hallucination staring out of the dark, my hair gleaming like silk. I stare until it's as if I belong among the faces who are part of the hotel's history.

'Oh, I bet you're pleased to see me.'

It's only Meryl, of course, ambling towards me with her comfortable gait and cheerful round face.

'Startled me,' I say.

'Off in a dolly daydream? I would say look sharp, Ros, if it weren't my turn to take over.'

Meryl's crinkled eyes help drain some of the enmity from the room. Her straw-coloured bob is limp with rain.

'Never like arriving when it's dark,' she says buoyantly, pushing wet strands out of her face. 'What with the history of this place.'

She means the deaths – some explained, some not – which have occurred over the years. We get paid more than your average receptionists.

'Do you believe it's really haunted?' I say. Villagers will swear up and down, but it's not like they'd know.

'Oh, there's something going on, alright, that's for certain.' Then, 'Any plans for the rest of the evening?'

'Nothing whatsoever,' I say, stretching my back out with a satisfying crack. I will walk out the front doors heading towards the car park, as if I'm going home. Then I'll loop around via the side path that leads to the back entrance and walk upstairs.

I moved in here soon after I quit university for good. Two years now.

'Not long now till the anniversary ball,' says Meryl, as I bend to pick up my bag. 'Peter seems to think that'll get this place back on its feet.'

'Let's hope so.'

'I certainly do hope so, because if it's not a success you and I could be out of a job!' Meryl shakes her head. 'Wouldn't have believed it if you'd told me twenty years ago the Crown Hotel was on the brink of closing.'

'It won't,' I say. 'It won't close.' As if saying it out loud will make a difference.

'We'll be stretched from pillar to post in the coming days, you mark my words,' says Meryl. 'I only hope they pay us extra for it!'

'Somehow I doubt it,' I say.

I've reached the front doors – I'll allow myself half a minute of fresh air, the taste of salt and the cry of airborne gulls, before retreating inside like a turtle to its shell.

***

Shouting rings from the back office, terrible as thunder. Another morning; it's cold enough to see my breath in front of me.

Julian's got someone in there – waitress, I think. His voice is loud enough to carry through the door. I tap softly at my keyboard. Intermittent words resound sharply: 'sheer laziness', 'moronic', 'useless'. I hear nothing from the girl. It carries on for several minutes until eventually the door opens. The waitress brushes by me at the front desk. Her eyes are red-rimmed, her face blotchy.

The door creaks open again. Heavy footsteps. I can hear Julian breathing over my shoulder and the hairs on the back of my neck rise.

'Good morning,' he says. His face is still red with the effort of anger but he smiles at me, forcefully.

Julian claims he could have gone professional in rugby, but the bulk of his body is going to seed. He's got a reddish-brown scruff of a beard and small, dark eyes that are almost black. Asked me out when I first started working here and I didn't know what to do other than say yes; we went on a few dates before I politely put an end to it. I try to keep him at arm's length.

'Morning,' I say, and turn back to my computer.

'Sorry about that,' he says. 'This recent crop of graduates don't know their arse from their elbow. I tell you, their generation just doesn't have the work ethic. Present company excluded, obviously.'

'I appreciate that,' I say, leaning towards my screen as though trying to read something important. Something whistles past my eyes and I startle; it lands on my desk with a harsh slap.

'Have a read of that,' says Julian. It's this morning's local paper – *The Crosswich Chronicles* – opened to a page midway through. Julian's finger jabs at a particular article. 'Go on.'

I begin reading aloud: 'Once a landmark destination and indulgent retreat for those able to afford it, East Yorkshire's historic Crown Hotel is, nowadays, more lacklustre than luxurious. Sadly, the hotel's staff appear to be floundering in their attempts to maintain –'

'Remember the critic who came in last week? Speccy bloke?'

'Vaguely.'

'Don't know how he thinks he can comment on much at all, to be honest. Dined in the restaurant before toddling off to bed at seven o'clock. No interest whatsoever in our other amenities. A drink in the bar would've been too much for him. You don't really drink, do you?'

'I don't.' It causes problems with my memory.

'Shame,' he says under his breath, thinking I can't hear him.

Then Julian's expression morphs into a fixed smile; he's looking at someone over my shoulder. I know who's at the desk before turning around.

'Morning, Peter,' Julian says.

Following Mark's death, Peter's now officially general manager – although he's acted the role long before his father's passing. A short, plump, ham roll of a man, Peter spends his day issuing edicts and invading personal space, all while self-consciously smoothing his comb-over. Childless, he divorced his second wife not too long ago; he likes to bring up her appearance as if he didn't willingly marry her. As if he's the epitome of male beauty.

I miss Mark's absently paternal approach – at least with his father in the building Peter's behaviour was a little more controlled.

'Hello, hello,' says Peter, leaning heavily over the front desk.

I smile politely but not encouragingly.

'What are we up to today, then?'

The obvious and only answer is 'work', but I'm spared answering by Julian.

'We've just been discussing that new review,' he says, shaking his head for effect. 'Isn't it terrible, how some people –'

'Ah, I don't give that paper the time of day,' says Peter. 'Only retirees and – now, what's the politically correct phrase – mentally challenged individuals?' He makes eye contact with me and winks, expecting me to laugh. 'Pay the *Chronicles* any attention. I think we can get by without their support, don't you?'

I'm not convinced we can. The hotel is struggling financially; everyone knows it. No-one's had a raise for ages and people are leaving in droves.

Peter leans forward and I can smell stale coffee on his breath. His teeth are yellowed from years of it sinking into the pores. Teeth have pores, you know.

'Quiet today, Rosalyn?' he says, another impossible question. He calls me Rosalyn because he knows I don't like it. 'Any chance of a smile and a nice "good morning"?'

'Good morning,' I say tonelessly. Animal instinct to escape, to go somewhere else. There's a world waiting for me outside these walls. That's part of what scares me.

'I'm counting on you over the next few days,' says Peter. 'There's a lot that needs doing in preparation for the ball, and I'm going to have to ask you and all the other…menial workers to pitch in.'

It's hardly a big surprise. 'That'll be fine,' I say.

'Knew you'd be happy to help. You've always been a good little worker.'

I'm taller than him, but I don't mention that. If I open my mouth there's a chance I'll vomit.

Peter drums his thick, stumpy fingers against the desk before slapping it once. 'Right-o. I'll leave you to it. Julian, I want that numbers report sent over in the next hour, if possible.'

'No problem whatsoever,' says Julian. It's a wonder he doesn't salute.

Once Peter's gone, I ask Julian, 'do you think the ball will raise enough to keep the hotel open?'

It's a touchy subject, but Julian manages our finances and I need to know.

He scrubs a hand down his face. 'Hard to say. My worry is it'll just go down as a fun night for the locals. Could be good for publicity, but the amount of money we need –' he cuts himself off, then smiles down at me. 'Nothing you need to worry about. Next door if you need me.'

There's nothing I could possibly need him for. He looks like he's gearing up to say something else and I try to mentally prepare myself.

'I'll let you get on, then,' he says. 'Those complaints won't resolve themselves.'
'No,' I say. 'They never do.'

CHAPTER TWO

I'm four rungs up a ladder, entangled in fake, decorative flowers. Preparations for the ball are underway, and my job is to drape the flowers over the wooden beam that supports the ceiling in the entry hall.

It's old wood, knotted and gnarled and chipped away. I shake out the string with my free hand before whipping it forward – the decorative blooms hang limply over the beam.

'Careful up there, Ros!' Meryl shouts, nearly making me lose my balance. Meryl's been helping paint a big canvas banner to hang in the ballroom. I'd rather have her job, but one of us needed to keep an eye on reception.

'Peter says he wants you in the ballroom,' says Meryl, settling down at the front desk. She'll open up a romance novel soon – Meryl owns an array of interchangeable paperbacks, each one stamped with the brooding image of a sailor, a policeman, a firefighter. I've tried to joke with her about it before, but she just smiles without understanding.

The ballroom hits with a wave of commotion. Usually empty and cavernous with its vaulted stone ceiling and tall, narrow windows, today the room is frantic. Round tables covered with starch-white tablecloths fill the front half of the room, with the rest of the floor free for dancing. Kitchen staff flit between tables, arranging cutlery, folding napkins into complex shapes, carrying boxes full of floral centrepieces. Balloons and ribbons are being fixed to cornices, silver and gold.

Meryl's banner is hung up on the back wall, where the stage is: *Crown Hotel's 175th Anniversary Ball.* The painted letters are just shy of looking amateurish. I could've done it neater. The room is full of bodies, of the clink and clatter of footsteps, plates and knives. There's barely space to move.

I can't see Peter anywhere.

A hand grabs my shoulder. 'Y'alright?'

'Don't do that,' I say, but can't help smiling. Arjun's too cosmopolitan, too intelligent to wait tables here for long, but I'll enjoy his company while I've got it. Cropped, bleach-blonde hair which contrasts with his dark skin, nose and ear piercings still in – even though when Peter notices, he'll have to take them out.

Some people don't care about upsetting the people in charge. It's not a luxury I have.

'What you doing in here, then?' says Arjun. 'Peter given you a job to do?'

'Yes, but I don't know what,' I say. 'Have you seen him anywhere?'

'Disappeared for a puff on his cigar. I wonder who he'll be voting for in the next election?'

'We can only guess.'

Nancy's loitering on the outskirts of our conversation. I smile at her because it's polite.

'Alright to join you for a sec?' she says. 'Not sure I can take much more of this lot!'

By 'this lot' Nancy must mean the kitchen staff, who are used to operating at a level of efficiency she's unfamiliar with. She works with me on reception. Until recently I assumed she was about thirty-five, but she's just a few years older than I am. Shoulder-length brown hair, round glasses – fond of a paisley blouse and sensible cardigan.

'How was your holiday?' says Arjun, and I try not to despair. Nancy's back from a family caravan holiday in the nearby countryside, something I heard far too much about even before they'd gone. I would say there's something depressing about taking a vacation in the same place you live, but then again I sleep where I work.

'Oh, it was just fantastic,' Nancy says, and I look up at the ceiling. Focus on details in the stone that have been the same for centuries and will continue to be the same. Some things are worth protecting.

'Rosalyn!'

Peter's plodding towards me – my heart sinks. 'There you are,' he says, as if I haven't been waiting for him to come back. 'I've got a special job for you.'

'What about the flowers at reception?' I say. 'Did you want me to finish that, or –'

'Oh, Nancy can take over there,' he says, waving a hand dismissively. When Nancy doesn't move, he says, 'well, go on.'

She ducks her head and scarpers.

'I'm sure you have jobs you could be doing, too, Arjun,' says Peter. His piggy eyes narrow into slits. 'Are those – this is your final warning. Take those fucking earrings out don't let me see you wearing them again. Just because you follow a certain lifestyle doesn't mean we all have to know about it.'

'Sorry about that,' says Arjun. He walks past Peter and does the wanker sign over his shoulder. I nod discreetly.

'Now then, missy,' says Peter, standing too close. 'As I said, I've got a special job for you.'

'What is it?'

'I think you'll like it,' he says. 'Should play into your artistic abilities. You studied art at university, didn't you?'

'History and Philosophy,' I say. Until I came home midway through final year.

Peter's watching me closely. 'Decided it wasn't for you, did you?'

'Something like that.' I shut my eyes and count two seconds, just brief enough to pass as a blink.

'You see that arch over there?' He places his hand on my shoulder and points. The bare, white bones of an unadorned archway have been set up, curving over the glass doors leading out into the gardens. His hand on my shoulder sends a lick of rage through me; I shift backwards and the hand grazes my back.

'You want me to decorate it?' I say.

'If you'd be so kind. The decorations are down in the basement, I'm afraid. I'm giving you full artistic license – you'll find balloons, flowers, fairy lights. Anything your heart could desire.'

'Right,' I say. 'How do you get down to the basement?'

'I'll show you.'

I slip my hand into my pocket to make sure I have my phone on me. Three quick presses on the power button triggers the emergency call. Although I'm not sure how quickly anyone could get to me down there. Not even sure there'll be signal if I need it.

'Come on,' he says, 'we haven't got all day.'

I expect him to lead me out of the ballroom but instead he marches towards the back of the room where the stage is. Peter manages to hoist himself up onto the platform with surprising agility, but when I get onto the stage he's breathing heavily, snorting through his nose. He leans on my shoulder for balance.

'Not as young as I once was,' he says, and then winks. 'More's the pity.'

I look around the room for a saviour or an ally, but everyone's busy and nobody looks up.

'I'll show you a secret way,' he says. 'Remember this.'

He draws aside the heavy red curtain that leads to the wings, then gestures for me to go through ahead of him. I don't want him walking behind me, but I can't just stand there. Hold my breath as I push forward into the darkness, as if that's going to do any good. It's almost pitch black beyond the curtain; as my eyes adjust, I can make out the shapes of strange objects.

'Just a storeroom,' says Peter. His breath is warm and damp on my neck. I shuffle forward and my foot bumps against something. There's nowhere for me to go.

'Where's the box?' I say.

'Right this way,' says Peter. He nudges a switch on the wall and paltry yellow light illuminates the room. It's filled with mannequins, faceless and stained with water damage. Some are wearing feather boas and pirate hats; others lie discarded on the floor, limbs in odd positions. Cardboard boxes filled with props – stools, tables and painted backdrops shunted against the wall.

'We used to put on plays, you see,' says Peter, moving carelessly past the fabric bodies. 'In the old days.'

He pushes open a door at the end of the room. It's dark and I can't see where it leads.

'Come on, I don't pay you to stand around and look pretty.'

I follow him; it feels like walking willingly into the jaws of a giant monster, further and further down the gullet.

There's a corridor on the other side of the door, narrow and crooked in a way that suggests it was built centuries ago and then abandoned. The walls are papered a peeling, sickly green and the roof slants over my head.

'Where are the decorations? Is it much further?'

'Patience, patience,' he says. 'The stairs to the cellar are at the end of this corridor.'

This does not fill me with reassurance. I don't like walking along this corridor, breathing in air that tastes of damp and decay, and I don't like following Peter deeper into the unpopulated parts of the hotel. Not that I could rely on people to do anything anyway. He keeps glancing behind him, checking I'm still there.

The staircase is wrought iron and very steep, spiralling down into darkness below.

'Watch your step,' he says cheerfully, again gesturing for me to go on ahead of him. I take a deep breath and hold it. What have I got on me, what's in my pockets? I search them surreptitiously as we go down – a ball point pen and a crumpled tissue. My room key, with its jagged teeth, is in my handbag. My handbag is at the front desk.

'You like it here, don't you?' says Peter. He's closer behind me than I thought.

'At the hotel? I do, yes.' I can't see where I'm putting my feet, holding the handrail and relying on instinct. The metallic clang of our footsteps is a dooming sound.

'And I like you being here,' he says. 'I'd never want you to feel beholden to me, just because I put you up for cheap rent. That means nothing at all; I do it because I want to. You don't feel you owe me anything, do you?'

'No,' I say, 'I don't.'

We've reached the bottom of the stairs.

'Light down here doesn't work, unfortunately,' says Peter. 'Have you got one of those light up things on your phone?'

'I'll turn my torch on,' I say. A white beam illuminates the basement one sliver at a time. The floorboards are old and rotting, and I swear I see the movement of something scurrying away from the light. Pieces of discarded furniture – a piano bench, a chest of drawers.

Peter's hand closes over mine, guiding the direction of my phone. My pulse spikes.

'There's the box,' he says, whisper-soft. His breath ghosts over my neck like the leathery wings of a bat. The bulbous tip of his nose brushes my hair. This close I realise he's a good head shorter than me.

I walk sharply towards the box, hoping to grab it and get out of here, but I soon as I bend over, I feel arms clamp around my middle. I cry out and try to pull away, rake my nails over his forearms but Peter's grip only tightens. I've dropped my phone, and it shines a glaring circle on the floor.

'I've been waiting to get you down here, Rosalyn,' he says, and somehow the use of my Christian name is the most diabolical thing of all. 'You don't know how I've waited...'

I can feel the erection tenting his trousers. I stamp down on his foot and he swears, shoves me forwards and I smack onto my knees. The edge of the box is digging into my stomach. His hands grab at my waist, pulling my shirt untucked, and I pick up something that has corners from the box. I twist round and swing the object towards his face; from its edges I realise it's shaped like a star. Peter howls. I take my moment. Snatch up my phone and then I'm running in the direction of the stairs. My hand closes around the railing and I'm taking the steps two at a time. I don't look back.

Keep running along the hideous corridor with its funhouse angles. Glance behind me and Peter's not following but I'm not slowing down. Hurt my shoulder banging into the door to the wings, my foot catches on one of those stupid mannequins and I hit the floor. I hear loud, gulping breaths and for a second I'm terrified I'm not alone, until I realise it's me making those noises.

I don't stay down for long; I pick myself up and breathe into my cupped hands until I'm calm again. Walk out of the wings with my head high and shoulders back. I won't be made a victim – I got away, didn't I? Climb down from the stage feeling like everyone's watching me, but of course no-one is.

The archway I was supposedly meant to decorate is still barren. People are occupied with their own tasks, the room filled with movement and voices. I don't want to look suspicious. A couple of metres away is a pile of balloons, already inflated and trailing with shiny ribbons. I don't know what they were originally meant for. Tug on the end of a ribbon and the balloon follows, like a bloated, floating dog. Rubber squeaks against my fingers and I feel it in my teeth.

Automatically, I begin tying the balloons to the archway. Lilac, pink, and yellow – I'll arrange them in a pattern. Pastel tones, possibly leftover from Easter. They don't match the colour palette elsewhere.

My hands are shaking too hard to tie a knot. I want to look busy, so nobody tries to speak to me. Puffed up and gleaming, the balloons look like dozens of fat, multi-coloured, laughing faces. I see them inflating larger and larger until they fill the room, jeering like a mob. Pressing me in until I can't breathe.

CHAPTER THREE

Every year, students are warned to not walk by the river at night. Especially while drunk. And every year, said the stern-faced woman on the morning of my induction, the university loses at least one student to drowning. In the autumn and winter months the banks flood easily, and the nights are very dark.

I remember thinking you'd have to be a moron to walk along the riverside when you can't see your feet in front of you. This helped assuage the fear struck into my impressionable heart, at least partly. You'd have to be stupid, I told myself. I'm not stupid. And I wouldn't make friends with stupid people.

It's three in the morning. I'm very drunk. There's a group of us walking back from a house party; bit of a wash-out, I thought, but I tried to look like I was enjoying myself. I'm walking with my best friend, Charlotte, a short distance behind the rest of the group.

'It's quicker this way,' someone yells over their shoulder. The bigger group splits off from the main road down a footpath, winding steeply downhill.

There are trees on either side. I follow them, not really paying attention because my best (and, if I'm honest, only) friend is crying. It hurts my chest and I don't know what to do about it.

'How could you?' she keeps saying. 'How could you?'

ACKNOWLEDGEMENTS

Thank you for reading this anthology from the 2024 cohort of the MA in Creative Writing Crime Fiction at the University of East Anglia. We were fortunate to be the first fully post-Covid students, able to meet in person for each residential, and to enjoy the beautiful green pastures of the campus.

As a group, our commitment to our projects was absolute as we interrogated ex-policemen, embarked on cruises, tested bottles of 'research' albariño and travelled to exotic locations, all in search of veracity. Weddings, flooded houses, RAAC panics and relocating across the world weren't enough to interfere with our dedication to show up at each residential, full of ideas and enthusiasm.

Throughout the two years, we were incredibly fortunate to have the expert guidance of Henry Sutton, Tom Benn and Nathan Ashman, ably supported by Stephanie Bishop, Jacob Huntley and Julianne Pachico. We owe them all deep thanks for taking us from raw, but enthusiastic scribblers in September 2022, to the writers presenting in this anthology today. Special thanks go to Henry for his kind words in the introduction to the anthology.

Along the way, we enjoyed masterclasses from Jill Dawson, Christabelle Dilks, Margot Douaihy, Louise Doughty, Nadine Matheson, Margie Orford and Laura Wilson. A special thanks must go to Louise, who kindly agreed to write the foreword to this anthology. We very much appreciate her generous contribution. Each speaker brought different experiences and insights, and offered the hope that we might, one day, be in their position, a successful author providing advice to eager students. A further treat was having the opportunity to examine the Lee Child archive in the UEA library under the guidance of Justine Mann and Elspeth Latimer.

Thanks to Juliet Mushens for preparing us for pastures new by revealing the steps to drafting an attention-grabbing submission package. Thanks also to the agents and publishers who sportingly tolerated our many questions. Sarah Helen Binney, Jamie Hodder Williams, Therese Keating, Hellie Ogden, Anna Power, Jack Ramm, Emma Shircliff, Euan Thorneycroft and Angelique Tran van Sang all graced us with their insights. A special shout out goes to Sphere Fiction Publishing Director Ed Wood, who also chairs the panel for the Little, Brown UEA Crime Fiction Award.

Thanks to the 2023 cohort for making us welcome at that first evening (of many) in the Garnet. It's wonderful to see them forging ahead in the crime fiction world, aided by their shiny new UEA degree.

Related to producing this anthology, we are particularly grateful to Emily Benton and Egg Box Publishing. Thanks are also due to the anthology committee – Kate Bailey, Elle Blair, Richard Jerram, Elaine Ruby and Van Stanley for editing and proofreading the contributions.

Finally, and most importantly, to all of our classmates – your support, encouragement, patience, and good humour have made these last two years life-changing. Thank you for being a bunch of all-round decent human beings. Best of luck to everyone in their future crime writing exploits.

UEA MA Creative Writing Anthologies: Crime Fiction

First published by Egg Box Publishing, 2024
Part of the UEA Publishing Project Ltd.

International © retained by individual authors

This book is sold subject to the condition that it shall not, by way of trade or otherwise, be lent, resold, hired out, stored in a retrieval system, or otherwise circulated without the publisher's prior consent in any form of binding or cover other than that in which it is published and without a similar condition including this condition being imposed on the subsequent purchaser.

A CIP record for this book is available from the British Library
Printed and bound in the UK by Imprint Digital

Distributed by BookSource
50 Cambuslang Road
Cambuslang
Glasgow
G32 8NB
+44 (0)141 642 9192
booksource.net

ISBN 978-1-915812-59-9